METAPHYSICS

AN ADVENTURE IN
SELF-DISCOVERY

Peter Dennis

CAPCO
INTERNATIONAL

ISBN: 0-9698926-5-9

Cover & Text design: Heidy Lawrance Associates
Printed in Canada

CAPCO INTERNATIONAL
7 Ashdown Crescent
Richmond Hill, Ontario
Canada, L4B 1Z8
Telephone: (905) 771-1543
Facsimile: (905) 771-9523
E-mail: **capco@interlog.com**
Web site: www.interlog.com/~capco

DEDICATION

I dedicate this book to those who are actively working to discover more about themselves. That's likely most of us, and it seems that learning about almost anything ultimately ends up in some form of self-discovery. This is both a never-ending adventure and one that is highly rewarding. I also believe that this is fundamental to our main mission in life and that this pursuit requires both courage and integrity. To those who actively pursue self-discovery, my hat is off to you, and may you enjoy the adventure as much as I have.

ACKNOWLEDGEMENTS

Most of the ideas and concepts presented here did not originate with me. Most, if not all, came from others whom I have been privileged to encounter, either in person, on tape, or in books. Some of these individuals and sources include: Deepak Chopra, Wayne Dyer, Brian Tracey, Gary Zukav, Srinivas Arka, Marcia Moore, Earl Nightengale, Laura Day, Dick Sutphen, Anne Morse, Shalila Sharamon, Bodo Baginski, Herbert Benson, Conversations with God, Bashar, Dr. Peebles, The Transeekers, Seth, Jesus Christ, and the list goes on. Some of my ideas are a blend of what I've read or heard and some are conclusions that I have come to after considering what others have had to say. In any event, I want to be clear that the ideas you will read here are not, for the most part, original and I am very grateful to the many who have contributed to my personal adventure in self-discovery.

As well, writing has always been a challenge for me and it was only with the editing of my wife, Carol-Ann Dennis and good friend, Elaine Charal, that I was able to get this book into final form. Thank you both very much.

INTRODUCTION

The purpose of this book is to advance our understanding of the infinite, consider how the universe might work and discover more about ourselves. Of course, as a finite being attempting to understand the infinite, I know that I've fallen considerably short. In recognizing that the concepts and ideas that I've expressed are by no means full or final answers, they can still advance our understanding. Although incomplete and sometimes flawed, these ideas are continually developing and evolving, and, for the most part, seem to work for me, at the present time.

As well, we are dealing with metaphysics, which is a cluster of principles and concepts, which, for the most part, cannot, at the present time, be empirically tested or proven. At best, one can choose to examine these ideas, embrace some and reject others, but, only as a matter of personal belief, not as a matter of science.

Science makes many contributions and validates much of what we experience in daily life but, when it comes to new ideas, it often needs time to catch up and learn to do the appropriate studies and measures. As we all know, at one time, science held that the earth was flat and that the sun revolved around it. It was only afterwards that it developed the tools to find otherwise. So today, you won't find much support for metaphysical ideas in current science although, interestingly, quantum physics and studies of the relationship between our thoughts and emotions, and our state of health are beginning to close the gap.

I also want to say that I realize some of these ideas fly in the face of certain organized religions and traditional thinking. Let me be clear: It is not my intention to offend or belittle any person, idea or organization.

Of course, if you don't like my ideas, you are perfectly free to reject them. My hope is that you will be intellectually honest with yourself and, if you do reject them, you will do so only after careful and fair consideration. If I differ with some generally accepted religious or philosophic principles or introduce ones that you haven't heard before, please allow yourself to consider them, think them through for yourself and come to your own conclusions.

I hope that some of these ideas will shake you a little and stimulate you to think in some new directions. I hope that, in your consideration, you will be analytical, listen to your intuition and decide what works for you. So far, these ideas work reasonably well for me. I have wrestled with them for years and they make more sense to me than most alternatives that I've encountered so far. I think I'm getting closer to some truths and I invite you to pursue and discover the truths that resonate with you.

Finally, although the ideas and concepts expressed here are my attempts to get at life's more profound truths, I hope that neither you nor I take our ideas or ourselves too seriously in this pursuit. These are only ideas and they are fallible and subject to change. I also hope that you will enjoy the intellectual stimulation and fun that can come from entertaining such ideas. So, let's see if we can have a little "intellectual fun" as we seek to understand the question that was raised in the song inspired by Michael Caine's character, Alfie, when it asked: "What's it all about?"

CONTENTS

1

THE UNIVERSE

This section is the foundation of the whole book. If you understand the ideas and concepts presented here, then the remainder of the book will make more sense. This may be the first time that you encounter some of these concepts and I recommend that you ponder them carefully, perhaps rereading some parts, before moving on to the subsequent sections.

WHAT IS GOD?

Likely, our first concept of God was something along the lines of an older, bearded gentleman who was wise, powerful and who somehow pulled the strings that orchestrated human affairs.

Over time, our concepts evolved and matured. We probably began to understand that God really didn't have a body, a gender or human limitations. Then, it began to get complicated. As our concepts matured, so did our questions. Where is God? What is His involvement with humans? How powerful is He? Where do we fit in? What are we supposed to be doing? Is He really pulling all the strings or is He allowing us the use of free will? What is the grand plan? Why did He create us, or anything for that matter? Is He perfect? Why does He allow evil? Did He actually create it? Does He change? Etc., etc.

Of course, organized religions provide some answers, as do mystics, gurus, scientists, preachers and others. Some tell us that they have the answers or their books do, or it is within each of us. Some say God is a being. Some say a force. Some say a spark of consciousness. It seems that the more answers we have, the more questions we develop. But, our concepts do evolve and we do edge closer, not likely to a final answer, but closer.

GOD IS ALL THAT IS

You will notice too, that God goes by many different names: God, Allah, Jehovah, Infinite Creator, etc. The one that I like best is:

"All That Is." It is a term that you see frequently in the metaphysical literature and it is one that I believe captures the essence of what God is. Many spiritual leaders, mystics, church managers, etc. tell us that God is omnipotent and universal. From this, I conclude that God is all — everything, everyone, everywhere, everywhen. God includes everything and everyone. There is nothing outside of God, including you and me. We are all included. We are aspects or expressions of God. We are a part of God and God is not separate from us.

GOD IS NOT A PERSON

As well, God is neither a person nor a being. It is too simplistic to personify God. We did this when times were simpler and we still do it today with children. God does not have a location, a body or a gender.

Another point: We often refer to God as He or Him but God includes both genders and is not limited by either. It would be more accurate, I believe, to refer to God as "It" but to many of us who use the English language, this is the pronoun we apply to inanimate objects or things that we value as less than human. That aside, I am going to use "It" when referring to God and I will intend at least as much respect as implied in personal pronouns.

I also believe that God does not suffer the human weaknesses of anger and ego. There are references in the Bible to God getting angry. As God includes everything and everyone, does it make any sense that God, in all of Its perfection, would be angry at Itself, or at any part of Itself? Isn't anger really unresolved frustration? Do we really think that God would be frustrated or incapable of resolving it? I don't believe for a moment that God is susceptible to anger.

As to ego, wouldn't it be a little like egomania to insist that One's creations engage in worshipping their creator? What possible need would God have for the worship of humans, again, which are a part of Itself? Isn't it more likely that the idea of worship is a human construct, perhaps the product of an organization engaged in the enterprise of leading large populations of worshippers?

So, if God isn't a person or a personality with human weaknesses, what is It?

GOD IS PURE CONSCIOUSNESS THAT INCLUDES EVERYTHING

Well, I believe that God's essence is consciousness and everything that exists, exists within that consciousness. I believe that that consciousness manifests as a force that includes and permeates everything and everyone, and holds everything together. There is no thing and no one that isn't included in God. Nothing can exist outside of God. There is no "outside of God." And, there is no separation from God, except by illusion — more about that later.

GOD'S PURPOSE IS TO EXPERIENCE AND CREATE

To get at this, let's go to the beginning. Of course, for God, there really was no beginning but there was for the physical universe. So, before the creation of the physical universe, God existed and God reflected on everything and, God being everything, God reflected on Itself. In this reflecting, God knew that it knew everything. That is, It had all knowledge of everything, actual and potential. It realized, however, that intellectual or cognitive knowledge was not as rich a knowledge as the knowledge that comes from experience. So, simply, God set out to experience all that It knew about cognitively.

As well, by nature, God is a creator, the infinite creator, and It could do nothing other than create. And, It did it from a twofold basis: One, unconditional love for Itself (meaning everything and everyone) and two, from a sense of fun. So, with this drive to experience all, with this natural creative urge, and with a sense of fun, God set out on a creating mission and It created a "playground" in which to experience all that It knew about cognitively.

GOD FRAGMENTS INTO POWERFUL PARTS TO EXPERIENCE LIMITATION AND SEPARATION

Now, being God, we would expect that It would not want to miss anything, so to cover all the bases, God fragmented Itself into powerful, parts or aspects. These aspects divided and the divisions subdivided and the subdivisions divided further and so on until we got to ourselves. Sub, sub, sub, etc., divisions or expressions of God. In this way, all of these subdivisions, aspects or expressions of God, could spread out, so to speak, to create, to explore and to experience every thing and every idea that actually or potentially exists.

As the subdividing went on, it eventually got down to us. It unfolded something like this: Imagine a group of powerful entities deciding what they would choose to create, explore and experience. Remember, these are powerful, creative, spiritual entities with no limits. What would be interesting for them? Well, they hit upon something that was very novel and different for them. They decided to pursue the idea of "Limitation."

Now, imagine if you were all-powerful, had no limits and wanted to experience limitation. How would you go about it? Well, one way would be to create an arena or a universe containing limiting elements, things like time, space and matter. In order to make it work, you would have to introduce one other key element. That is, if one was truly unlimited and was going to experience limitation, one would have to somehow put aside or "forget" one's true unlimited nature. So, this forgetting process was invented for all of those who incarnate into this universe. That is, everyone born into this universe "forgets" his/her true nature in order to experience limitation and "play the game." We have to. Otherwise, how could we truly experience limitation if, all along, we knew that this was really just an illusion that we had created and the real us actually had no limits? We couldn't play the game fairly, could we?

Now, in addition to being unlimited, God was also unified, meaning, all was one and one was all. In deciding to experience limitation, God also decided to experience the opposite to unification, namely, separation. To pursue this idea, God/we have created the illusion that all isn't one or that you and I and God are all separate from one another. Just to intensify the impact of this illusion, we created a universe of polarities, e.g. black and white, up and down, hot and cold, positive and negative, male and female, etc.

SUMMARY

So, here we are, aspects of God, creating, playing and experiencing in a realm or universe of limitation and separation. And, we are doing this while other aspects of God are busy experiencing other universes with other conditions and circumstances that they have created for the purpose of experiencing other ideas that God knows cognitively but not experientially.

WE ARE MULTI-DIMENSIONAL AND HOLOGRAPHIC

Now, given that we are essentially powerful, unlimited aspects of God creating this physical universe in order to experience all that we can in a universe of limitation and separation, how could we do this fully? Remember there are only limits once we incarnate but there's an incredible, unlimited intelligence behind the creation of this experience that makes it all work and enables us to get the most from it.

To get the most from it, it was decided to make the beings experiencing it, namely us, multi-dimensional. Why restrict experience to only one dimension when the possibilities are so much greater? We are multi-dimensional in at least two ways. First, we live many lives simultaneously but, in our "limited" human minds, we separate them in time so that they appear to be past, present and future lives. That is to say, at a level "higher" than ourselves, we create many personalities. That is, our higher self fragments into many aspects, each of which takes on its own personality and is born into a different time period. Some are male some female, some are rich, some poor, some are nice, some rotten, etc. until that entity has enough aspects to engage in all of the experiences that it wishes.

Here's where the plot thickens. The second way we are multi-dimensional is that, each time we come to a decision point, we fragment further to explore all of the alternatives. For example, if we decide to get married, we do and we don't — we experience both. One aspect of us goes one way and another goes another. Further, if we do decide to marry, we could marry any of a number of potential partners and, so, we do. Each of our person-alities, of course, is not aware of this or the others because our consciousness is limited and focused only in one personality at a time. From the perspective of our higher self, it is all happening simultaneously and the higher self is experiencing all of the possible experiences and variations that it has set out to experience.

Bashar provides an analogy that has helped me to understand some of this. He speaks of a projectionist and a filmstrip. The filmstrip has a number of frames and, from the perspective of any one frame, there are frames that come before it and others that come after. Each frame can represent a lifetime, with the frames on one side representing past lives and the frames on the other side representing future lives. From the perspective of the projectionist, however, the frames can all be viewed at once. Similarly, from the prospective of the oversoul or higher self, the lifetimes are all happening simultaneously.

Additionally, we are holographic, which means that each one of us contains all the information of the whole. That is, we have all knowledge but, of course, have chosen to forget it or put it aside while we are exploring limitation and physicality.

SUMMARY

We are unlimited, multi-dimensional, holographic fragments of God (souls) creating the illusion of a physical universe in order to explore the concepts of limitation and separation, with the purpose of learning experientially what we know cognitively and, to accomplish this with integrity, we have chosen to temporarily forget that the real reality is one that is spiritual, unified and unlimited.

WE DENSIFY ENERGY TO CREATE THE ILLUSION OF A PHYSICAL UNIVERSE

Before the physical universe, the unified consciousness (God) or "All That Is", as I stated, decided to fragment and experience all that It was aware of cognitively. One of the ideas that It decided to pursue was "limitation." This meant creating a universe of matter, time and space. The souls or fragments of God who pursued this idea, had to create two things, a physical universe in which to experience and play, and a mechanism for forgetting who they really were, namely beings without limitation.

In creating this physical universe, God/we had only consciousness to work with. Consciousness includes thought, self-awareness and unconditional self-love. These combined to produce the creating energy of our physical universe. As our scientists are telling us today, our physical universe is made up mostly of space that contains a vibrating energy force. They refer to this force as the unified field. When the vibration is slower, the resultant illusion is one of more solidity or denseness. When it's faster, it is lighter and more spirit-like.

On earth, we live with the illusion of a physical universe. As creators, we have created a wide range of vibrational frequencies, some of which result in illusions of physical reality while others result in illusions that are non-physical or spiritual.

Density, then, refers to a specific illusion or apparent reality that results from a particular vibrational frequency. As creators, we decided to expand our range of experience by creating a great many of these illusionary realities. Each of these realities has its own unique vibrational frequency and we refer to them as the different densities.

Although there is a vast number of different densities, we commonly group them into seven clusters that we refer to as the seven densities. These are broad categories that include all of the densities while giving us a convenient model with which to organize, understand and describe them. The seven densities, some physical and some spiritual, are described as follows:

FIRST DENSITY

- Consciousness is one-dimensional.
- The frequency of physical matter.
- The densest of the physical levels.
- Minerals, elements and compounds exist here.
- Provides the matter and energy of atoms and molecules.
- Also found in the human genetic code.

SECOND DENSITY

- Consciousness is two-dimensional.
- The frequency of plants and animals.
- Development of group or species identity.
- Self-awareness (ego) not developed.

THIRD DENSITY

- Consciousness is three-dimensional.
- Humans exist here and are currently moving into fourth density. As we do, we experience accelerating (faster vibration) change and individual breakdowns.
- Individual identity (ego) develops here.
- Consciousness here includes recalling the past, thinking about the future, while being aware of the present.
- The illusion of separation is strongest in this density.
- Dolphins and whales exist here as well as in fourth density.
- Primates exist in this density as well.
- The pace of individual realities is stepped up resulting in more rapid and intense personal issues and change.

FOURTH DENSITY

- Consciousness is Superconsciousness.
- Consciousness takes on group identity without any loss of individual identity.
- The perception of past, present and future begins to blend.
- Consciousness extends to multidimensional and multidensity realities.
- Negatively oriented consciousness becomes more difficult to maintain.
- An attitude of responsibility takes hold here.

- This is the last frequency for physical bodies.
- On earth, fourth density is overlapping third and we see more desire for peace and harmony.
- The illusion of separation begins to diminish.

FIFTH DENSITY

- This is the first density of non-physical reality.
- It is not limited by time.
- In this density, individuals have an urge to share the wisdom of this consciousness with those of the lower densities.
- Many in this density become guides for others in lower densities.
- Fifth density beings merge with their oversouls or higher selves.

SIXTH DENSITY

- This is the density of the "Christ Consciousness," the frequency of Christ or Buddha.
- It is the density of angels.
- In sixth density, beings recall their true identity.
- Here, the interest of the whole is seen as completely consistent with the interest of the individual.

SEVENTH DENSITY

- Consciousness is multi-dimensional.
- This is the frequency where all become one consciousness. That is, limitation and separation dissolve and all become one integrated whole, ready to move on to other adventures.

Note: For the descriptions of the different densities, I have borrowed heavily from *The Prism of Lyra*, pages four to seven, by Lyssa Royal and Keith Priest. They have done a marvellous job in making these clear and I thank them.

SUMMARY

So here's what's been covered so far:
- God is not a person separate from us but pure consciousness, manifesting as a force that is in everything.
- God has no gender, location, ego, or limits, nor does It need or want the worship of humans.
- God is everywhere, everywhen and everything. It includes all of us as well as all things. There is nothing outside of or separate from God.
- God's purpose is to create and It does so because that is Its nature and because It wishes to experience all that It knows cognitively.
- We are multi-dimensional, holographic aspects/fragments/ expressions of All That Is (God).

- We, as a fragment of God, with the full capability of God, are exploring and experiencing different things, in an infinite number of ways, so as to contribute to the overall experiential learning of a higher aspect of ourselves (our oversoul) and ultimately, All That Is/God.
- As we experience and play in this universe of limitation and separation, through many lifetimes, and evolve through the levels of density,
  - We move away from the illusions of limitation and separation.
  - We push back the veil of forgetfulness
  - We expand our awareness
  - We recall more of what we truly are
  - And, thus, we progress back towards the unlimited and unified consciousness or source from which we originated.
- To create this universe, we work with energy and we densify it to varying degrees. The seven major degrees or levels of density are primarily for:
  1. Minerals, elements and compounds
  2. Most species of plants and animals
  3. Humans, primates and cetaceans
  4. Humans, peace and Superconsciousness
  5. First level of non-physicality
  6. The frequency of Christ, Buddah and angels
  7. Total oneness and integration
- As we evolve through these levels of density, we are heading home and, because we end up with the understanding that comes from the experiencing of all this, God is richer for the experience.

- As parts of the Infinite Creator, We, have been creating the whole time. This is inherently the nature of God. We have been creating our personalities, our universe, and our whole experience. We are the Creator. Creating is what we do.
- And, because creating combined with learning experientially is what we do, then once done, we start off on other adventures, in other universes. And, I'll leave it to you to imagine what that's all about.

2

SOME OTHER PIECES TO THE PUZZLE

In most cases, the metaphysical principles presented in this section follow from and build upon the ideas presented in Part 1. I hope you will find them thought provoking and that they will stimulate more thinking and investigation on your part.

BELIEF

This one used to anger me a great deal. I encountered it quite fully in Bashar's book: "A Blueprint for Change, A Message from Our Future." This is a great book, channelled by Daryl Anka and full of wisdom, insights and good explanations. What angered me was that it repeatedly said that if we wanted something to change or manifest, all we had to do was believe it would and it would.

What angered me was the idea that it was portrayed as being so easy. If I wanted a new car, all I had to do was believe that I had it and I would have it. But how could I easily adopt that belief if all my prior experience told me that it doesn't happen that way? Apparently, everything in our reality is based on belief. If we believe our bodies will deteriorate, as we get older, they will. If we believe that they won't, they won't. As someone once said: "If you believe that something will happen or if you believe that it won't, you're right."

Of course, if we live with other humans, we cannot help but embrace the collective beliefs of the masses. So, even if we try to believe that our bodies don't have to decline as we age, at some level, the collective belief will impact us and compromise our personal belief. It is nearly impossible for us to counter the collective beliefs. As a result, we believe that the sun is harmful and so it harms us. Or, we believe that we should die generally before reaching 100, so most of us do. For a long time, we believed that it was impossible to break the four-minute mile but, once it was done, many others did it, and almost immediately afterwards. Belief is everything.

There are degrees of belief. We can think that something might be true. We can believe that something is true. And, we can know profoundly, deep in our bones, that something is true. Knowing is the most powerful and, of course, sometimes the most difficult to hold.

We might liken it to riding a bicycle where we can think that we won't fall over, where we believe that we will stay up or where we just know, at the deepest level, with absolutely no doubt, that we will stay up.

The trick is to have this absolute knowing and completely hold the belief, and then the reality will follow. We cannot have the slightest amount of doubt. The tiniest bit will be enough to undermine the whole belief structure and render it ineffective.

So, how do we embrace a belief that flies in the face of past experience? I think there are three ways that can make it happen. One, ignore or remove ourselves from the limiting beliefs of others. This is just about impossible for most people except, perhaps, for the hermits among us. Two, employ supporting affirmations that will condition us to adopt a new belief. Much like the old brainwashing technique where, if you say it enough, you come to believe it (saying is believing). And three, we can simply act as though we fully hold the belief. This isn't always easy, and there probably are limitations but there is evidence that people, who conduct themselves with confidence, do attract success.

Anyway, consider the proposition that, believing is seeing and not the other way around; as we are commonly lead to believe. Consider affirming the desired reality and conducting yourself as though the desired reality is already present. Try this as an experiment and monitor the results.

As a suggestion, you might consider experimenting with wealth or abundance. Continually tell yourself that you have everything that you need and that you are the grateful beneficiary of abundance. Behave as if you have more money and other material possessions than you need. Be generous and donate to charity and to the less fortunate. The old saying, "What goes around, comes around" is well established as one of the fundamental rules of the universe and you can put it to the test.

As well, don't forget, that abundance or wealth does not only come in the form of money. Often it can show up as that free ticket that comes our way, the unexpected discount that we receive, the surprise opportunity for a bargain or simply a gift.

Abundance is only one way that we can experiment with this idea of belief. Another is to play with our outlook on life. We all know of people who seem to have a rosy outlook and for whom life seems easier. As well, we know others who cannot find anything much good to say about life at all, and guess what kind of life they attract?

One might argue which comes first, the reality or the outlook, but I suggest that, if we start with the outlook, the corresponding reality will show up. Try it and see what works for you. If there is a part of your life that you are not happy with, try affirming and expecting the kind of life that you do desire and see if, in time, it doesn't begin to take form and develop.

REINCARNATION

Most people on planet Earth believe in it. Most organized religions either embrace it or at one time did. Even in the west, where today most churches no longer believe in it, a great many individuals do anyway. The New Testament gives us reason to believe that it was generally held in Christ's day when it portrays Christ's apostles asking him if he was Moses, Abraham, Adam, etc.

In the fourth century, when Christianity became the official religion of Rome, Emperor Constantine deleted references to reincarnation from the New Testament. In the sixth century, the second council of Constantinople officially declared reincarnation a heresy. Reference: "Reincarnation: The Phoenix Fire Mystery" by Cranston & Head.

Why is Christianity the apparent exception? Well, one speculation is that the Church fathers decided that their interests would be better served if the faithful believed they only had one lifetime in which to achieve salvation. They were afraid that if the faithful knew they had many lifetimes, they might be tempted to stray from the straight and narrow during this life, knowing that they could always recover during subsequent ones.

What makes sense here? Of course, this depends on what you believe about God and Its purpose. If you believe, as I do, that God's purpose is to create and experience all that is, then it seems illogical that we, as fragments of God, would limit ourselves so as to only experience things through one personality when the alternative of multiple personalities is just as easy and the rewards are so much richer. Why would we choose to do it just once?

Well, I don't believe that we do. What I believe happens is that, in our natural, spiritual state, we plan each physical lifetime and we plan each one with other souls who will play support roles. For example, in a given lifetime, we would plan and arrange agreements about who our parents will be, who main players such as family members, spouses, spirit guides and people of greater influence during the life will be. Each time we find ourselves between lives, we spend a certain amount of time planning and arranging such agreements.

This brings up the question of free will. If we have an agreement, for example, to marry someone and raise children with him or her, do we really have free choice about marrying them or not? I believe that we do have the freedom to choose not to go through with the agreement but, chances are, that what motivated us to strike the agreement in the first place is still operating and we will feel compelled to enter into the marriage. If we choose not to, chances are that we will engage in other activities that will bring about similar experiences and lessons as the original agreement was intended to. Either way, we will end up with the sought-after experience and learning opportunity.

Another way of putting it is that, if we agreed that we will go down a certain path, then we will go down that path but we are free to go down it dancing, running, doing cartwheels or dragging our heels, but we will go down that path. So, in summary, we do have the free will to make the agreements and plans, we do have the free will to execute the plans in any of a variety of ways but it is probably not easy to choose to abandon a plan and never encounter the experience or lessons that we have agreed to pursue.

A final word on reincarnation: Some souls choose to incarnate literally hundreds of times while others may do it only once. It depends on one's purpose. Bashar claims to have done it only once so that he would have a better feeling for the nature of humans, as one of his purposes is to interact with them as a fourth/fifth density being through trance channelling.

LAWS OF THE UNIVERSE

Bashar says there are only four laws of the universe. He is talking about the whole universe here, not just earth and not just in this physical realm. The four laws are:

1. We exist. We always have and we always will. We will not die, our bodies will but we will go on, forever.
2. All is One, One is All. This means that God is everything and everyone. God is all and, therefore, all is God. We are all part of the whole. No one is excluded. God is not separate from us. Nothing is separate from anyone or anything. We are all one.
3. What you put out is what you get back. This is also known as the Law of Attraction, which states that we attract whatever we think about, be it positive or negative. What we put out in thought and action comes back to us.
4. Everything changes except the first three laws.

That's it. These are the immutable laws upon which the universe functions.

CHANNELING

I have a few friends who go into a light trance and allow another entity to speak through them. This is a very loving and cooperative arrangement and in no way is a possession or an involuntary "Take over." You have probably heard of trance channelers. Some of the entities like Seth, Lazarus, Dr. Peebles, Bashar or the Transeekers are quite famous. Their channelers have appeared on talk shows, before large audiences and also conduct private sessions.

Whether these channelers are actually channeling another entity or are somehow accessing another part of themselves, such as their subconscious, I believe two things are true. One, the channeler believes that another entity is coming through and two; the information that is spoken is usually very good. Long ago, I concluded that it probably doesn't matter what is going on as long as the information makes sense, is helpful and is offered in a loving manner.

The content can be anything from the origins of the universe and how the Creator works to how to deal with personal illness or problems in relationships. In my experience with channeled information, I have always found it interesting, logical, intelligent and delivered in a direct, caring and helpful way. So, I really don't care very much where it comes from. I am just grateful for the content and the assistance it provides.

My favourite channelers are Darryl Anka who channels Bashar, Thomas Jacobson who channels Dr. Peebles, Dale Landry who channels Dr. Smithson and a number of others, Barbara Marciniak who channels the Pleiadians, Anne Morse who channels the Transeekers, Lyssa Royal who channels several entities who provide information on the origins of the universe and extra-terrestrials and Neale Donald Walsch who, through automatic writing, channeled the books: "Conversations with God."

For years, I have been somewhat in awe of channelers and have wanted to do what they were doing so that I too could facilitate the flow of useful information. I have read books that were channelled, I have read books that explained how one could learn to channel and I have asked channeled entities how I might do it. As well, I have been quite frustrated in not mastering the technique when some of my friends do it with apparent ease.

Well, I'm getting closer. I've been told that nearly everyone can channel and that most people actually do in one form or another. I haven't found this latter statement all that consoling but I'm beginning to understand how this can be true. Most of us have moments when information, inspirations, solutions, etc. just seem to pop into our heads. These, I'm told are channeling moments.

At first, I wasn't convinced that this was channeling. I felt that these were simply thoughts that came from within myself or came bubbling up from some portion of my unconscious mind. The Transeekers explained to me that some of these thoughts may, indeed, be my own but that many were coming from elsewhere and were examples of channeled information. I asked how someone could distinguish one from the other and they gave me a little exercise that sorts it out.

They asked me to close my eyes and answer the question: "What is my name?" I did and they asked me to locate the position in my head where the answer seemed to come from. I responded, upper, centre left. They then asked me to close my eyes and note the location of the next response. This time they had a question for my spirit guides who they said were gathered around me. They asked the guides, "Are you with Peter" and asked me to relay their answer, yes or no. I immediately answered, "Yes" and reported that the response seemed to come from the upper right side of my head. They pointed out that I now knew the difference. Information coming from others, outside of myself, could be discerned by feeling the direction from which it came. If it came from the upper right region of my head, it was from someone else.

This, they explained, was a form of channeling. People do it all the time. Another example, that you may recall, is from the movie Amadeus, where Mozart was near his death and he couldn't write fast enough to capture all of the information that was flowing through him? Have you ever been "in the zone" where the ideas just gushed forth? I have to say that, right now, as I'm writing this, the words are coming more quickly than I would have thought and my two fingers are typing more quickly than usual. I think this is happening because writing this information is something that I'm supposed to be doing and the ideas, words and fingers are flowing better and faster than they would normally.

However, as interesting and as productive as this flow may be and as this is one form of channeling, it still isn't the same as someone sitting down, going into trance and then starting to speak with an altogether different speech pattern and bringing forth information that they wouldn't normally produce by themselves. If you haven't seen trance channeling for yourself, I suggest that you seriously consider taking the opportunity when it next presents itself. I doubt that you'll be disappointed.

SPIRIT GUIDES

When we are between physical lives, we make a number of agreements with others in order to orchestrate the next life so that it fulfills its intended purpose. For example, we form agreements with those who will play significant roles in our more important activities and relationships, such as parents, siblings, friends, helpers, etc. As well, we form agreements with certain individuals who agree to stay in the spirit realm while we live in the physical world so that they can be around to provide us with guidance, inspiration and insight. These we refer to as spirit guides.

We all have spirit guides. Generally, we each have one principal guide and we then have others who come and go to help us with particular challenges, at particular times.

How do we receive information from our guides? Well, they communicate with us all the time but we often ignore the messages or we dismiss them as just another idea coming from our mind or imagination. And, as we do get messages or ideas from our mind and imagination all the time, how can we tell which messages are coming from ourselves and which are coming from our guides?

One way is to use the technique outlined by the Transeekers in the section above on Channeling where you notice where in your head or body the information is coming from. Certainly, it helps if you believe that you have guides, talk to them frequently and build a relationship. If we practice paying attention to these messages, intuitions, etc., and note where in the body they come from, and then act upon them, we can learn when an idea is valid and in our best interest.

For example, I have a friend who knows when a message is valid because her right forearm tingles whenever she gets a valid idea. This took years to recognize and validate but it is now a reliable tool for her.

In my case, when I get a flash idea, inspiration, hunch, etc., if it comes from the upper right of my head, I believe it is from my guides and I pay attention. When such a flash comes from elsewhere, I believe it comes from my mind or imagination. I also pay attention to ideas and information that comes from my mind or imagination but it's useful to know the source.

Another example: One day Carol-Ann was in a large retail outlet and noticed that one of the buckles was missing from one of her shoes. She was sure that it had detached while she was in the store. I focused on it for a second, and got an upper right flash that it was lying on the floor in the back corner of the store. I went directly to the spot and picked up the buckle. Was this from some unconscious part of my mind? Perhaps, but either way, this insight was useful and I choose to credit it to one of my guides.

ANGELS

We each have a guardian angel. These beings come from the sixth density and are thus from the spirit dimension. They are assigned to humans in order to help us in day-to-day affairs and, as many of us were told as children, they can keep us from harm.

Angels have the ability to manifest physically and appear as other humans. We sometimes hear stories of individuals who show up at critical times to avert a danger or to help someone through a difficult set of circumstances.

By way of example, I have a friend who swears that an angel helped her in a moment of need. She found herself in a rather dangerous part of town when her car broke down. She was quite distressed as the neighbourhood had a bad reputation for violence. As she was sitting and fretting in her car a young man on a motorcycle pulled up to her window and asked if he could help. He seemed pleasant enough and she trusted him immediately. She opened the hood of her car and, in short order, he got the car going. For a moment she was distracted and looked the other way. When she turned back to thank the young man, he was gone. To this day, she maintains that it would have been impossible for anyone to drive away on a motorcycle and not be seen in that amount of time. Her explanation is that the young man was an angel.

Whether she is right or wrong, this is typical of angel stories.

JUDGEMENT

We are told in the Bible and by church leaders: "Judge not lest ye be judged." Contrary to what many believe, this does not mean that if you judge others, God will judge you and you will somehow be punished for having judged someone else. What it really means is that if we engage in judgement, we will set up a vibration of judgement that will boomerang on us. It will be a drain on our energy and it will impede our progress. Judging others creates a no-win situation for ourselves. We do not rise by putting others down.

More important, how can we judge another when we really don't know what their agenda is or what they are supposed to be doing in their current life? Until we know their life purpose, we cannot. When we see what we might call "Bad" behaviour, we are certainly entitled to decide whether we view this as positive or negative, or whether or not it is behaviour that we prefer or wish to adopt, but we are in no position to determine or judge if it is the appropriate or inappropriate behaviour for that person, at that point in his/her life.

Remember each of us is living out our life, seeking to experience certain things that are unique. Some of these experiences are what we often term "Negative." But, we have to experience the negative in order to know the positive. We are in a universe of duality. We must have up to know down. We need hot to know cold. We also need "Evil" to know "Good." I put quotation marks around these words because they are only labels that we assign from our perspective. In the absolute, there is no "Good" or "Evil." All is just experience that we are gathering so that, in total, we will come to know all experientially rather than only cognitively.

So, if we don't know an individual's purpose, we are in no position to judge the individual because they may very well be on their way to achieving their purpose. Yes, we can judge their behaviour and decide if we like it or not but our best course is to love the individual, remembering that they, like us, are part of the whole that we call God.

GRATITUDE

It seems that those of us who are thankful for and take pleasure in life's events, circumstances and material things, have a more upbeat and happier life. For example, I run a little over five kilometres every third day or so. Sometimes this is not easy, especially when running into a strong headwind or when the legs are tired and sluggish. However, when I finish each run, I reflect on how fortunate I am that I can do this and I thank God for the ability to do it. This seems to enhance the joy of the event and of the resultant feelings of fitness that it fosters. Taking that moment at the end of the run to feel that sense of gratitude really enhances the experience as well as provides the motivation to do it again.

I'm finding too that there are many daily opportunities to feel that same sense of gratitude. They can happen when you are having a conversation with someone and you feel how fortunate you are to have that encounter and to have experienced that person's greatness. This attitude helps us to search for, find and appreciate the many wonders of creation.

If we are truly thankful for the many encounters of the day, we seem to take the time to pay attention to them more, appreciate them more and simply enjoy them more. Life seems to unfold in a much more positive and pleasant way.

In "Conversations with God," God says that the best prayer is one of gratitude. If we thank God for a particular event, achievement, acquisition, etc., we will set up the vibration of having it. And that will attract it more likely than the expression of a want. If we tell God that we want something, the likelihood is that our request will be granted and wanting is what we will get. Not the object of our want but the want of the object.

Expressing gratitude sets up the feeling of gratitude. With that feeling, our approach to the world is more positive and joyous and we end up with a more positive and joyful reality. It behooves us to adopt "The attitude of gratitude."

INJURY, DISEASE AND AGING

Most, if not all disease is rooted in our emotions and thoughts.

In our daily lives, as we continually encounter challenges and opportunities, we react by making decisions about them. These decisions are made either out of love or out of fear. One is the opposite of the other.

If the decision is love-based then love flows and emotional harmony results. From this harmony, growth follows, our energy is in balance and our immune system is strengthened. This results in wellness and fulfillment.

On the other hand, when fear wins out and our decisions are fear-based, fear flows and emotional disharmony follows. This leads to feelings of distress, putting our energy out of balance and weakening our immune system. Illness results and, if serious enough, we are headed for a system breakdown.

If at any time after making a fear-based decision, we wish to exercise a love-based alternative, we can do so and thus reverse the flow of fear and restore the love flow to the system, thus producing a state of wellness.

Here are some love-based motives: caring for others, caring for ourselves, commitment, confidence, courage, decisiveness, enthusiasm, forgiveness, generosity, honesty, humility, intimacy, integrity, interdependence, loyalty, respect for self, respect for others, responsibility, self-confidence, trust and truth. When these drive our decisions, they are love-based.

Some fear-based motives would include: abuse of self, abuse of others, anger, avoidance, defensiveness, denial, desire for attention, doubt, guilt feeling, hatred, indecisiveness, jealousy, judgement, resentment, self-consciousness, self-underestimation, sensitivity to criticism, stinginess, vanity, withdrawal, worry. When these drive our decisions, our decisions are fear-based.

So, to stay healthy, we need to make sure that all decisions we make are based in love and not in fear.

Now, of course, this is not easy. It is not easy because our motives are based in our underlying beliefs and controlling our beliefs is a major challenge that is nearly impossible. If the collective belief is that the sun's rays are harmful, then, at some level, because that belief is expressed all around us, then we will likely incorporate that belief and it will then colour all of our decisions about exposure to the sun. For example, if we find that we have been in the sun longer than the collective believes is safe, we will begin to suffer some skin damage.

So, in summary, if our beliefs foster love-based emotions and thoughts, then we are on the road to wellness.

SLEEP

Sleep is required for the body, the spirit and the human species. It is our way of connecting with these aspects of ourselves and with the infinite. One of life's myths is that, as we age, we need less sleep. We don't, we need more. As a species, at this time, we need more than we used to. We need it for a number of reasons.

As a species, we are in transition. We are evolving into a new density, often referred to as the fourth density. This evolution is well under way and much of the work is being done in our sleep state.

We need sleep for the spiritual part of ourselves. One school of thought says that the spirit finds this material dimension of limitation extremely confining and must simply get out and about regularly. Sleep affords the spirit that opportunity.

And, our physicians tell us that our bodies need sleep to regenerate, heal and strengthen.

Most insomniacs are controlling individuals. They feel that they cannot let go of consciousness and allow their unconscious selves to deal with the issues of the day. They feel that they must be awake and always working on life's challenges. They find it difficult to let go of this idea and trust that, in a sleep state, their mind can be addressing and resolving daily issues.

One idea for countering insomnia was provided by a friend who said that, before falling asleep, she would visualize all of her daily problems on the floor, dissolving into dust. She would sweep the dust into a box and put it on a shelf to be dealt with when she awoke the next day. A variation of this idea might be, that while visualizing the problems in this box, one assign them to the unconscious mind by simply requesting that the unconscious mind work on the contents of the box while the individual is sleeping and thus give oneself permission to sleep longer so the unconscious has sufficient time to do this work.

As well, if we realize that important work is also being done for the evolution of the species during sleep, then there is further valid reason to allow oneself to sleep longer.

EXTRATERRESTRIALS

Extraterrestrials exist in a different density than the one we occupy. That's why we cannot see them and, until we raise our vibration collectively, as a species, we never will. As well, our scientists can continue to spend billions on space probes, satellites and listening devices but it will be to no avail. It's like searching for birds underwater. They just don't exist there.

Birds will sometimes venture underwater, however, just as ETs will sometimes lower their vibration and become visible to us. They are doing this and their purpose is to get us ready for broader contact. But that isn't going to happen until we become more civilized as a species and then, collectively, our vibration will rise so that we will exist in the higher density.

We are currently in the third density evolving into the fourth. ETs are generally in the fourth and fifth. Once we stop killing one another, end our wars and become civilized, we will be contacted and invited to join the Federation of Civilizations. Until then, the ETs really don't want much to do with us. On the other hand, they are doing much to help us.

Extraterrestrials have intervened frequently to prevent us from blowing ourselves and our planet up. They have helped us to advance our technology. This is evidenced by the fact that we have advanced far more technologically in recent years than we have in previous centuries and I suggest it is naive to think that we suddenly acquired the ability to do this all by ourselves.

KARMA

Karma means balance. The soul being multi-dimensional and having many incarnations, seeks a perpetual state of balance. So, if in one life, we are particularly oppressive to others, the soul will incarnate into circumstances where we can be oppressed and thus the two will be in balance with each other. Karma is the innate force of the soul that seeks to always be balanced.

PREDICTING THE FUTURE

We create our own reality and, in so doing, we decide our own future. Technically, no one can predict our future until we decide it. We may not decide it at a conscious level, but at some level, we do create our own future, and sometimes, at an unconscious level, in cooperation with others

When fortune tellers, tarot readers and other seers predict our future, they are really just picking up on the trends that are currently happening in our lives, extrapolating them into the future and identifying the most probable outcome.

We can change this most probable future at any time if we choose to. Most often, we don't and our most probable future then comes to pass.

To illustrate, someone may ask a fortune-teller: "Will I be wealthy?" Most fortune-tellers are not aware of how their gift works and they only see the most probable outcomes. So, in this case, one may tune in to the individual and pronounce that he/she will become wealthy. If, however, the fortune-teller is consciously aware of what she/he is really reading, then she will see that a number of forces are trending in the wealth direction and will access that the probabilities are 70% that the individual will become wealthy. He/she will then explain that the most probable future for that individual is one of wealth and will possibly acknowledge that the seeker can change that outcome at any time.

EMOTION

One of our main missions in life is to learn about ourselves. This seems consistent with the idea that we are each different and are out to experience what we can through the personality that we have chosen for this life. If you accept that we are supposed to learn about ourselves, then you probably have to acknowledge that much of what constitutes the self is our emotions.

The subject of emotional intelligence has been made popular by the research of Revuen BarOn, the writing of Daniel Goldman and the contributions of others. The research is telling us that Emotional Intelligence is about three times more important than Cognitive Intelligence for success in life and for success in the workplace.

Emotional Intelligence can be defined as all of those emotional and social skills that contribute to success. It includes emotional self-awareness, empathy and optimism, among others. The good news about emotional intelligence is that it can be grown and developed. And, growing it is consistent with our mission of learning about our emotionality and thus, about ourselves.

From the perspective of athletics, isn't it the emotions that separate the great athletic performances from the good ones. Athletes are always talking about how they feel, how motivated they are, how driven and determined they are, and how heightened emotions make the difference between winning and losing, breaking records and establishing personal bests.

It is our emotions that drive us to new heights, push us through challenges and take us to new places. They are so fundamental to what we are. And, when we learn about our own emotional makeup, we are truly and more deeply learning about ourselves.

How do we learn about our own emotionality? One way is to measure some of the components. There are some popular instruments around for doing this. The BarOn EQ-i measures emotional intelligence, probably better than any other instrument. By getting a measure of our different emotional components, we can get some feeling for how our emotions compare to the norms or to general averages. Next, we can find books, exercises, etc. that help develop the different emotional components and we can observe our progress and development. Being the observer of this process will heighten our awareness and sensitivity to our emotional makeup.

3

SOME THOUGHT STARTERS

Here are twenty ideas that I find interesting and deserving of further consideration. For each, I offer three questions that I hope will prompt you to investigate further and come to your own conclusions.

BIRTH AND DEATH

Recalling the first law of the universe — we don't die, our bodies do but we go on forever — in a sense, birth and death are the same thing. Birth is passing from the spiritual realm to the physical while death is reversing the process, going from the physical to the spiritual.

- Which of the two do you think is the more difficult process?
- Why do we fear death?
- Do you think we might also fear birth?

WORLD POPULATION

We seem to sometimes worry about over-population. Perhaps, we worry needlessly as, presumably, there are a limited number of souls (maybe, a little over six billion) willing to incarnate into this third density reality on planet Earth.

- Do you think that the number of souls interested in Earthly existence is unlimited?
- What do you think of the idea that some souls are only interested in experiencing the womb or the birth channel, and does that change any of your thinking about abortion?
- Under what circumstances would over-population be possible?

THE EARTH AS A SENTIENT BEING

Many peoples, over the centuries, have held that the Earth is a sentient being. Some have referred to it as "Mother Earth" and ascribe a level of respect to it that exceeds the common regard of today. Wouldn't it be interesting to see how differently we would all act if we truly believed that the Earth was alive, thinking and feeling?

- Could our eco-system be a respiratory system?
- Could Earth's waterways be a circulatory system?
- If it is a sentient being, what could the Earth's agenda include?

HEROES

Those who choose to incarnate into this third density reality are held by many in the spirit world to be heroes. That's because of all the struggle and difficulty that we choose to take on. This idea can give one the perspective that, the more a soul engages in illness, handicaps and other strife, the more that one truly is a hero. It might change the way we look at some of those around us who are living in the most misery and who are struggling with the most difficult challenges. They are the real heroes.

- What might the lessons be for one who decides to incarnate as a mentally handicapped individual?
- What might the lessons be for those who come in contact with such an individual?
- Could such people be giving the rest of us a gift, such as an insight, a lesson or an opportunity?

THE OBSERVER

Our outlook on life would be different if we adopted the perspective of the observer. This is an ancient concept where one would mentally detach from what is going on and look upon it as another, objective individual might. For example, imagine that we are working to meet a tight deadline and the stress is mounting. If we can mentally step outside of ourselves, look down, and think: "This is interesting. I wonder how it will turn out," we become more detached and less caught up in the tension of the moment.

- If you could assume the perspective of the observer, what benefits do you think might result?
- In what kind of situations do you think it would be practical to be the observer?
- In the heat of a stressful moment, how would you remind yourself to assume the role of the observer?

THE DISAPPEARANCE OF THE DINOSAURS

The dinosaurs likely did not disappear because of a giant meteor hitting the earth or a flood or some other such disaster. They, along with other large, grotesque creatures were the first attempt to populate the Earth. The ones responsible for the task of populating the Earth did not like their first attempt and deemed it a failure. They then set out to retrieve all of the specimens in order to start over. A few individuals "slipped through the net" so to speak, and, today, we still have a few examples, the Sasquatch,

Bigfoot, the Yeti and possibly Ogo-pogo and the Lock Ness Monster.

- In light of all the reports of sightings and with the lack of absolute proof, do you think the existence of such creatures as the Sasquatch, the Yeti, etc. is possible?
- What do you think about the idea that a species of powerful beings could be responsible for populating the Earth?
- If there was such a species with this responsibility, do you think they might have done it with a single Adam and Eve or with many prototypes? And, where does evolution fit in?

LEMURIA

This was an ancient civilization that existed about 80,000 years ago. It was a continent situated in the South Pacific and slowly, over a thousand years or so, sank. During this time, the planet was predominately intuitive and feminine. Lemurians had very developed technology and knew that their continent was sinking. Knowing that their days were numbered, they migrated away to as far south as Peru and as far north as California. As Lemuria sank Atlantis rose and many of the former Lemurians went to Atlantis and started to colonize it.

- Do you think it is possible that there were ancient civilizations populating Earth before our current recorded histories?
- Do you notice a shift going on now where the planet is becoming more feminine and intuitive?

- Do you think it is possible that such an ancient civilization could have had technologies that were more advanced than some of our present day technologies?

ATLANTIS

Atlantis was an ancient civilization that existed about 50,000 years ago on a continent between Africa and the Americas. The people were more advanced than we are and had nuclear capability, which they failed to control. They eventually blew themselves up, the continent's pieces sank and the reverberations through the universe have caused some of the Extraterrestrials to never allow such an event to happen again. Lately, there have been a few ET interventions to prevent nuclear explosions on earth.

- Could the existence of Atlantis account for the many similarities in architecture, e.g. pyramids and temples, between those found in Mexico and Central America, and those of Egypt?
- Do you think with all the radical factions on Earth today, it is likely that we will blow ourselves up again?
- What do you think has prevented it so far?

THE MAYA

Today, some scientists are trying to explain the almost total disappearance of this once mighty race. The answer is that they simply moved on to fourth density, having had enough of third.

- What other explanations could account for the disappearance of so many of the Maya?
- What could account for the Maya's advanced understanding of mathematics and their sophisticated calendar?
- What do you think of the idea that Alantians had an influence on the early Maya?

PLAY

Any species, to the degree that we can observe, seems to engage in play, e.g. kittens, cubs, children, etc. I suspect that those species where we cannot measure or make this observation, play, to some extent anyway. I wonder if this isn't a reflection of the Creator who, I also believe, has a sense of play, has created a large playground for us and who creates with a sense of fun.

- Why don't adults play as much as children?
- What is the importance of play in human affairs?
- How can we build more play into our daily routines?

TELEVISION AND MOVIES

We see themes of Extraterrestrials and metaphysics being played out more and more in the movies and on television these days. This isn't entirely by accident. Creativity abounds in these media and it is here that inspirations are played out for the purpose of exposing us to these themes and preparing us for their reality.

- Movies such as *Close Encounters of the Third Kind, Contact,* and some of the Star Trek movies seem to be examples of movies that are preparing us for the reality of ETs and metaphysics. What other movies can you think of that are also "Preparing the way?"
- Where do you think the creators of these movies get their ideas?
- In the movies and on television, what are some of the common themes and trends that are emerging?

CLIMATE

Our climatic conditions are a function of our collective consciousness. If we, as a species, are violent and raging, that is how our weather patterns will behave. If we are peaceful and tranquil, then that is what we will experience. These days, we seem to have individuals and groups operating at both ends of this spectrum and our weather follows accordingly.

- What climatic or weather changes have you noticed lately?
- Do you think that, apart from pollution, there could be anything else that accounts for these changes?
- What might it take to one day control our weather conditions?

WHALES AND DOLPHINS

Cetaceans operate on a much more emotional level than we do and, from the perspective of Extraterrestrials, they are the other sentient species on planet Earth. You may recall the Star Trek movie where ETs were attempting communication with Earthlings and were making contact with whales rather than humans. The thesis was that whales were more developed and telepathic communication was easier with them.

- What do you think about whales and dolphins in captivity, e.g. Marineland?
- Why do you suppose humans get such a "kick" out of swimming with whales and dolphins?
- Why do you think whales and dolphins bother to interact with humans?

DOMESTIC PETS

When you see a pet with a physical ailment, look to see what is going on in the life of its owner. Often, pets will take on some of our diseases and provide, not only relief from the disease's effects, but an opportunity for us to see more clearly what changes need to be made in our lives.

- Think of a pet that is afflicted with a degenerative disease. What is going on in the life of the owner that might bring on such a disease?
- In such a case, what changes in the owner's life might ease the disease?
- Why do you think cancer patients are often advised to get a dog?

ILLNESS AND DISEASE

An illness or disease contains a message. For example, a cold is a message to slow down. If we don't pay attention, the body will send pneumonia or something else that will make the point. Next time you are sick, examine what's going on in your life. There is a reason for the illness and, if we are wise, we can discover it. Louise Hay writes and speaks extensively on this subject.

- Think of the last time you had a cold. What was your life like then?
- What changes did you have to make in order to get rid of the cold? What was the lesson here?
- Sometimes, at an unconscious level, we take on an illness so that others can learn a lesson. Can you think of an instance where you or someone else sustained an injury or illness and others around them learned something valuable, e.g. caring for others?

ASTROLOGY

Don't discount Astrology. I don't mean the pop-stuff that you see in the newspapers' daily horoscopes but the real study that has been with us for centuries, long before astronomy. The planets and stars all vibrate, as does everything in the universe. Vibrations travel and affect everything else. Is it so preposterous then that the vibrations sent out by such large bodies as the planets and stars would have an effect on humans and on human affairs? As the moon affects tides and some human behaviour, shouldn't we be open-minded to possible influences from Mars, Jupiter and the others?

- What has your experience been at times of a full moon? Have you noticed any differences in human behaviour, including your own?
- Have you noticed any trends in sun signs, e.g. are you attracted to people born under certain signs, do athletic champions seem to be of certain signs, have you noticed common body traits in some signs?
- Have you ever seriously examined the track record of predictions of some of the more prominent Astrologers?

CHRIST CONSCIOUSNESS

This is the level of consciousness that exists in sixth density. Entities from it visit our third density world from time-to-time to intervene and to nudge us along. Jesus Christ, Buddha and angels are examples.

- Do you believe that angels influence us in our every-day affairs?
- As we are all aspects or expressions of God, do you think that Jesus Christ was any more the Son of God than any one of us?
- If we can believe the stories, Christ was likely our greatest manifestor, e.g. wine from water, loaves and fishes, etc. What accounts for this ability?

A SCHOOL OF PATIENCE

Don't you get the idea that much of what we do here on Earth is somehow designed to teach us patience? Raising children, working with others, dealing with mistakes, ours and other people's, all seem to be opportunities to learn to be patient. Interestingly, as we learn this lesson, there is a payoff. Things fall into place more easily, relationships are more harmonious and stress levels are lower. Perhaps, one of the reasons we are here is to learn about patience.

- Do you recall times when you were angry with someone else only to realize that the anger was really with yourself?
- As opposed to the old saying: "Haste makes waste," can you recall instances when approaching a situation calmly and patiently led to a more efficient and enjoyable result?
- Is a patient response versus an impatient response always a matter of choice?

A SCHOOL OF RELATIONSHIPS

This Earth experience has often been referred to as a school. If it is a school, perhaps more than anything else, it is a school where we experience and learn about relationships.

- When you think about some of life's biggest lessons, what has been the role of relationships?
- Generally speaking, would you say that those who succeed best in life have done so mainly because they are good at building and maintaining relationships?

- What is the correlation between the strength of a relationship and the effort that one puts into developing and maintaining it?

SELF-DISCOVERY

As we are each an aspect of God, looking for unique experiences, we find that there are no duplicates. God doesn't need to experience anything more than once. Hence, there are no duplicates, humans, animals, snowflakes or anything else. Put another way, if we were all identical, there would only be a need for one of us.

So, with each of us being unique, we each have a unique personality and our mission is to explore our life experience through the lens of that personality. We are, in effect, on a mission of self-discovery and it can be therefore said that our Earth is a school of self-discovery.

- How effective is learning about others in teaching us more about ourselves?
- Do we learn more about ourselves in our successes or in our failures?
- If God is on a mission to learn experientially and we, as a part of God, have taken on a unique personality to share in that mission, does it then follow that we should be learning all that we can by personally experiencing as much as possible?

4

MEDITATION

Meditation is a means of dissolving the barrier between the conscious and unconscious portions of our minds and of getting more directly in touch with our greater self. It has many physiological benefits and it helps us to get closer to what we really are. In a search for self-discovery, it is a valuable tool and, in this section, we will explore what it is, what the benefits are, how to do it and how, in a state of meditation, we can enhance visualization, affirmations and goal achievement.

WHAT MEDITATION IS NOT

First, meditation is not a life style; it is not about religion, philosophy or contemplation. You don't have to wear sandals, sit in contorted positions or make strange sounds.

The practice of meditation has been around for millennia. Although it has been a part of yoga and certain religions for centuries, it wasn't until the late 1950s, that Maharishi Mahesh Yogi introduced Transcendental Meditation to the West. With people like The Beatles, Hans Selye, Deepak Chopra, Clint Eastwood, Joe Namath and Governor Gerry Brown embracing it, meditation began to take root in our part of the world. Shortly after, Dr. Herbert Benson of Harvard did much to "legitimize" meditation when he published the results of his research in his popular book, *The Relaxation Response.*

The term meditation is often extended to include pleasant thoughts or themes that can be contemplated. For example, you hear of "Meditations for Teachers," Meditations for Reducing Stress," etc. These can be pleasant and productive ideas to contemplate or mentally dwell upon but they are not meditation. At best, they may be ideas that can be entertained in a state of meditation but they are not, in themselves, meditation.

WHAT MEDITATION IS

For our purposes, meditation can be defined as a simple, natural and effortless process for achieving a state of deep relaxation while the mind remains alert and aware. It is something that is very peaceful and enjoyable to do.

In sleep, we can also achieve a state of relaxation but our mind is not conscious and we are not aware. As well, we may not be all that relaxed — especially if we are being chased in our dreams by a lion or tiger. In meditation, our metabolism slows down significantly and our brain wave pattern changes from a waking state of approximately thirteen to twenty-six cycles per second (this is called beta wave activity) to a frequency of approximately eight to twelve cycles per second (alpha). These two changes signal the state of meditation and result in a great many benefits.

WHY MEDITATE?

Among the many benefits, regular meditators find increases in such areas as academic performance, athletic performance, cardiovascular efficiency, creativity, emotional stability, energy level, interpersonal relations, job performance, learning ability, metabolic stability, nervous system efficiency, perceptual ability, resistance to disease, self–esteem and sociability.

Regular meditators also report decreases in the use of alcohol, cigarettes and non–prescription drugs, as well as decreases in excessive weight, heart rate, high blood pressure, anxiety and depression.

Meditation produces benefits for nearly everyone. On an individual basis, adults, teenagers and children can benefit from it.

On a group basis, it is ideal for work groups, social groups, executive committees, clubs and anyone who is interested in improving their competence, happiness and quality of life.

In summary, meditators look younger, are healthier, handle stress better and enjoy life more.

HOW TO MEDITATE

Meditating is easy. Finding the time to meditate, on a regular basis, is the hard part. Most meditators find a regular time and most find the morning, before they start their day, to be best. There is also a fair number who meditate just before their evening meal and some who like to meditate in the evening just before bedtime.

The answer as to when to meditate is very individual and I recommend that you experiment, taking into account your daily schedule and how meditation affects you. For example, some people prefer to meditate just before bedtime as it helps them to sleep better while others find that meditating in the evening energizes them and makes sleeping difficult.

To induce the meditative response in the nervous system, we need to place our attention on a single action or object so that our mind begins to still itself and cease jumping around from thought to thought. We do this by placing our attention on a mantra. A mantra can be a word, a sound, or an object. It might be musical notes, a symbol, one's breathing, someone's voice, a setting sun or a candle flame. When we place our attention on a mantra, the mind quiets and the meditative state is induced. It's that simple.

What mantra works best? This, again, is very individual and I suggest that you experiment until you find one or two that you prefer. I do suggest that when starting out you use a mantra that involves having the eyes closed so as to protect against visual distractions.

What seems to work well with many beginners is a word that is linked with one's breathing. Words that work well are "one," "in," and "out." The way in which you would use these would be to think (not say or even whisper but just subtly think) "one" each time you inhale and/or exhale. Some prefer to link a word only on inhalations, some only on exhalations and some on both. You have to try the different combinations and come to the one that works best for you. In my case, I find that thinking "in" on each inhalation and thinking "out" on each exhalation works best.

An important point to remember is that the mind cannot be totally controlled. At best, it can be tamed. What typically happens in meditation is that one is focused on one's mantra and, after a few moments, the mind wanders from the mantra to some distracting thought or idea. This is normal and it is important to relax and realize that this is normal and not "beat oneself up" over it. Just simply and gently come back to the mantra and carry on focusing on it. When the mind wanders again, once again, just bring it back to the mantra and carry on. Pretty soon, perhaps, after five minutes or so, the meditation response will kick in and you will be meditating.

A SIX-STEP PROCEDURE

To ensure that you induce this state, here is a simple six-step procedure:

1. Select a quiet environment where you know you won't be disturbed. Disconnect telephones and advise others that you wish to be undisturbed for the next 20 to 30 minutes or so.
2. Sit in a comfortable position, back straight, feet flat on the floor, hands in lap, eyes closed.
3. Assume a passive attitude — empty the mind of all thoughts and distractions.
4. Select a mantra and focus on it. When you notice that your mind has wandered to a thought, just gently come back to your mantra.
5. Continue until you wish to stop. Fifteen to twenty minutes is enough for many people but sometimes it is attractive to stay in the state longer. Don't force anything, just be comfortable.
6. Open your eyes slowly. Take a full twenty to thirty seconds to open them fully.

SOME ADDITIONAL POINTS ABOUT MEDITATION

- Some people prefer to sit on the floor or to lie down. Both are fine and each has a risk. When sitting on the floor, it is important to ensure that the spinal column is straight. When lying down, there is some risk of falling asleep. This isn't bad but it's not meditation.

- If you raise your eyes about 10 degrees while they are closed, you can induce the meditative state more easily.
- It is important that you are not disturbed or that noises such as a ringing telephone or slamming door don't occur during meditation. You will soon notice that, in the meditative state, your senses are heightened and that you hear things more acutely. When an unexpected noise occurs, you will find it somewhat startling or jarring.
- During meditation, all bodily processes slow down, including digestion. For this reason, it is important that meditation is not done on a full stomach. Otherwise, the lump of undigested food sitting in the digestive track becomes uncomfortable and distracting. When meditating, it is a good idea to let a couple of hours go by after eating.
- Opening the eyes slowly after meditating is important. Otherwise the light rushing in can be a little jarring to the eyes.
- The amount of light in the room while meditating is, again, a matter of individual preference. Experiment until you find the level of lighting that you prefer. Most people prefer some reduction from normal daylight but the preferences do span a wide range.
- Soft, upholstered chairs can sometimes be too soft and not provide the proper amount of support to maintain a straight spinal column. Often the best chairs are straight backed and fairly firm in the seat. Dining room chairs are usually pretty good although they may take a little getting used to.
- For the first few times, when sitting up straight, you may find

your head tending to fall forward or backward. By adjusting your body forward or backward, you will come to a balance point where this soon becomes a non-issue.

- While in meditation, with eyes closed, it is common to see visuals. These can range from vivid objects and scenes to simple colours. This is normal and usually quite pleasant. Don't be alarmed, just enjoy.

- Sometimes, especially when a little sleep-deprived, we relax so much that our brain wave activity falls to Theta, four to eight beats per second. Theta is the brain wave activity that accompanies dreaming. It can happen that while you are meditating a little dream scenario will flit by. Again, relax, this is normal and fairly common. You will notice too, that much like dreaming in sleep, we rather quickly lose the recall of these meditation dreams. As well, we will probably be a little mystified as to what they had to do with anything we were thinking or doing in our waking life.

MEDITATION AND AFFIRMATIONS

The old brainwashing techniques of the 1950s taught us that if you say something often enough, you will eventually come to believe it. And, when we believe something to be true, our unconscious mind is busy finding ways of making it true.

The unconscious mind is not judgemental, it just accepts what it is being told and acts upon it. It is the processor while our conscious mind is the programmer. The thoughts and ideas that the programmer (conscious mind) chooses to run is the program and the processor (unconscious mind) runs them.

Some scientists have said that we generate thousands of thoughts every day, most of which are negative or worrisome. If our unconscious mind is processing mostly negative thoughts is it any surprise that the resultant reality is mostly negative?

We can change that. We can choose the thoughts that we run through our conscious mind for the greater unconscious to process. If we choose pleasant, positive thoughts, then the resultant reality will be pleasant and positive. It's our choice. Don't we all know people who constantly revel in negativity? And what kind of reality do they get? As well, we all know people who are continually upbeat and positive and they seem to live in a much more positive reality.

Also, back in the 1950s, we heard Earl Nightingale's classic lecture, "The Strangest Secret." The lecture lasted for about twenty minutes but the essence of it was that *we become what we think about most of the time.*

And, so it is with affirmations. These are positive statements that we can formulate and then repeat to ourselves. Doing so in a state of meditation enhances their power because, when meditating, the barrier between the conscious and unconscious mind is lessened and the impact of whatever program the conscious mind is running is greater.

SOME EXAMPLE AFFIRMATIONS

- I like myself unconditionally, without reservation.
- I always speak positively about myself and others.
- I enjoy and appreciate everyone I meet. I like them and they like me.
- I always decide for myself what is best for me and I allow others the same right.
- I accept complete responsibility for my life and for all of my actions.
- I enjoy excellent health and I am easily able to relax at any time.
- I am always calm, confident and self-assured in my interaction with others, with groups as well as individuals.
- I am very creative in all areas of my life, always tapping more and more into my unconscious mind.
- I have an excellent memory and I can easily recall names, numbers and other information.
- I am a total winner and am completely successful at anything I do.

Note: I copied these affirmations quite a few years ago and have changed some of the wording since then. I believe I found them in some of Brian Tracey's material but cannot recall exactly where. In any event, I am a great fan of Brian Tracey and I thank him for these ideas and I highly recommend that you check out his seminars, tapes and books.

There is a variety of ways affirmations can be handled in meditation. Certainly, while meditating, one could not recall very many. Perhaps, you may only wish to deal with a few at a time.

Alternatively, you could tape record a larger number and play them once in a state of meditation, or you could have a friend read them while you are meditating. In that case, he/she would have to change the pronouns from I to you.

In any event, experiment with affirmations when in meditation and consider using them at other times as well, e.g. when driving in the car. Remember, when we say them, we are running a new and positive program that the unconscious mind will pick up and process. Remember too, the strangest secret: *We become what we think about most of the time.*

MEDITATION AND GOALS

I have often thought that, if I ruled the world, I would see to it that every citizen had the opportunity to learn how to meditate and how to set and achieve goals. I really think that, if this were the case, it would be a very different world. It would be much more peaceful, individuals would be more satisfied with themselves and we would all enjoy life a whole lot more.

THE POWER OF WRITTEN GOALS

To illustrate the power of written goals, one has only to recall the quintessential research that was conducted in 1953 where a number of researchers asked a question to all of the graduating students at Yale University. The question was: "Do you have written goals? Guess how many said yes? No, it wasn't half the class. It wasn't a quarter. It wasn't ten percent. It was three percent. Only three percent of the 1953 graduating class at Yale University had written goals.

In 1973, 20 years later, the researchers caught up with as many of the 1953 graduates as they could and, this time, they had a battery of questionnaires and surveys for them. Their first finding was that the three percent who had written goals had a total net worth in excess of the other 97 percent who did not have written goals. Many speculated that, this being the case, probably, they weren't happy. Not true. The three percent outscored the 97 percent on every scale surveyed, e.g. job satisfaction, quality of life, relationships, recreation, etc.

This research has been replicated many times. The jury is in. There's no doubt, written goals work. Those with written goals succeed better than those without.

So, how does this work? Well, there's two parts: Goal Setting and Goal Achieving. Goal Setting works best when certain principles are followed. One way to develop effective goals is to follow the format outlined by the acronym S.M.A.R.T.

S.M.A.R.T GOALS

S stands for Specific. By specific I mean that we spell out exactly what is to be achieved. For example, we could have a goal that reads: *I will increase sales*. To make this goal more specific, we might state: *I will increase unit sales of XYZ product*.

M stands for Measurable. Wherever possible, it is wise to quantify our goals. In our example, we might say: *I will increase unit sales of XYZ product by 25%*. It may not always be possible to quantify every goal but, with a little thought, it is often surprising how often this can be done. For example, we may have the very valid goal of increasing morale. But how do you hang a number on morale? Well, you can certainly place numbers on some of the correlates of good morale, e.g. attendance, timeliness, good quality, etc. These, then, might become candidates for goal statements rather than morale.

Measurable also means to place a timeline on our goals. In our case, the goal could now read: *By December 31, 2002, I will increase unit sales of XYZ product by 25%*.

A stands for Attainable. The idea here is that achieving worthwhile goals usually takes us outside of our comfort zone and into territory that is new and, sometimes, a little scary. We want to challenge ourselves, on the one hand, while ensuring that the goal is within realistic reach, on the other. We want to strike a balance between challenge and realism.

R stands for Relevant. The energy that we place behind our goals is very much a function of the relationship between our goals and the things that we value most in life. Goals are effective when they relate closely to our values. Effective goal setting requires a solid grasp of the goal setter's values and then ensures that the goals are consistent with them.

T stands for Trackable. If our goal were to increase sales by 25% within a year, then wouldn't it be prudent to check, say, each month or so to see how we are tracking? For example, if after three months, we found that we hadn't increased sales at all or that we had increased them by 20%, shouldn't we revisit the goal and perhaps make an adjustment? Effective goals have milestones along the way so that appropriate adjustments can be made.

SOME ADDITIONAL POINTS ABOUT GOALS

- It is a good idea to write a goal out fully and then edit it until we feel we have a statement that is clear, concise and accurately describes exactly what it is that we want, no more, no less.
- Goals are better written in cursive. As our world becomes more digitized, we lose certain brain activities. Education kinesiologists tell us that cursive writing, certain cross body movements, some dance and the martial arts help to restore and develop some of these abilities. I believe there is a certain power to impact the unconscious mind that cursive writing has that printing and typing don't have.
- Goals can cover all aspects of our lives. Consider goals for:
  - Meaningful work or purpose
  - Wealth and abundance
  - Physical and emotional wellness
  - Loving relationships
  - Charitable giving
  - Intellectual development
  - Play and recreation
  - Spiritual development

- Goals can be short term or long term. Some literature refers to the longer term (greater than one year) as goals while shorter-term targets are referred to as objectives or outcomes. I don't believe that the terminology matters so much as the recognition that goals range considerably in the time they take for accomplishment and that some goals are achieved only when other shorter-term goals are met.
- Remember the Law of Attraction: We attract the things we that think about. So, think about your goals frequently.
- Once a goal is thought about, expect that it will show up.
- Strongly desired goals are more likely to be achieved than those that we are rather ambivalent about. When stating a goal, it is a good idea to ask why we want it. This will lead to the motivation behind it. And, if the motivation is strong, then there will be more energy behind it and it will be more likely to be accomplished.
- It is a good idea to state our goals out loud a few times each day. We can do this when we have private moments, e.g. in the car. Failing this, we can read or state them silently. Either way we are keeping them in mind where they are being recognized, assimilated and worked upon.
- Having copies of our goals placed around our home, office, in the car, etc. where we are bound to see them frequently keeps them in our conscious mind and therefore in the processor of our unconscious mind.
- One idea for achieving goals that is worth experimenting with is to consider the goal as already achieved. For example if your goal is a new car, visualize yourself as enjoying the

new car. As well, when viewing the goal as already achieved, be grateful for it. In Conversations with God, God says that the best prayer is one of gratitude.

- Whether you imagine the goal as already achieved or not, when visualizing the goal, employ the senses and the emotions. In the example of a new car, imagine the smell, feel, sound, etc. of the car and use you emotions to feel the joy, satisfaction, exhilaration, etc. of driving the car.

SUMMARY

To achieve goals, they must be clearly articulated, strongly desired, thought about frequently, expected, and action must be undertaken.

HOW WE SABOTAGE GOAL ACHIEVEMENT

Now, these steps by themselves are not enough for most of us. It seems that most of us, often at an unconscious level, have one or more undermining beliefs. These beliefs are usually one or more of the following:

- I don't deserve to have this goal so easily.
- Achieving this goal will change me into an unlikeable character.
- I won't be able to handle it.
- I just don't believe that it will be achieved.

If we are entertaining any of these, they will undermine all of our efforts. If you discover or suspect that any of theses apply to you, then you can reverse them by using affirmations. For example, if you think that, at some level, you don't deserve wealth that comes without having to work hard for it, you might try repeating affirmations like the following:

- I deserve large financial windfalls that come easily to me.
- I deserve wealth that comes easily to me without having to work hard for it.
- I deserve to be wealthy.

If we can eliminate all undermining beliefs and doubts, then strongly desiring a goal, thinking about it and taking action will bring it about.

So, how does all of this relate to meditation? Well, like affirmations, when goals are contemplated in a state of meditation, the barrier between the conscious and unconscious minds is weakened and the unconscious mind is impacted more strongly. It is the unconscious mind that processes what we consciously tell it and brings our thoughts into reality. Simply, thinking about our goals in a meditative state, is a more powerful way of projecting thought.

MEDITATION AND STRESS

Meditation has been called the ultimate stress reducer. Certainly, one of the claims that meditators make is that it reduces stress dramatically. As well, meditators seem to be calmer than most folks and they don't seem to age as rapidly. Let's examine this a little.

A FEW POINTS ABOUT STRESS

- Stress is the tension state that the nervous system produces when we react to something that we see as a challenge or threat. The key word here is "react." Two people can be in exactly the same set of circumstances and one will react calmly while the other will get agitated and upset. Consider, for example, a traffic jam where there can be a whole range of reactions, some of which result in stress.
- Stress can be positive, helpful and necessary if we are to meet challenges and deal with threats. Imagine, for example, the start of the Olympic 100 metre finals and one athlete has absolutely no stress. I suggest that the race would be mostly over before that athlete reacted to the gun and started running.
- Stress turns into distress when it becomes damaging and unpleasant. Dr. Hans Selye wrote the book: "Stress without Distress" and made this important distinction. Stress is positive and necessary, while distress is negative and dysfunctional.

THE FIGHT-FLIGHT RESPONSE

When we produce distress, the nervous system triggers:

- An increased respiration rate
- An increase in the heart's throughput of blood
- An increase in brain alertness
- A restriction of blood vessels in certain muscles
- An increase in kidney activity
- A secretion of adrenocorticotrophic (ACTH or stress hormone) from the pituitary gland
- A secretion of adrenalin from the adrenal glands
- A secretion of cholesterol from the liver.

This is known as the fight-flight response and when it is activated, all of these reactions kick in. In a life-threatening situation, where running or fighting is required, this is a useful response as it gets the body ready to react in one or both of these ways.

In today's world, however, where the situations that bring distress are not life threatening, we nevertheless elicit the response and the chemicals flow. If we do not run or fight, the chemicals pool and, after a while, when this has happened over time, the conditions are right for hypertension to set it, thus leading to heart disease. This is one reason why aerobic exercise can be so important — it can blow off the chemicals and clear out the pipes.

MEDITATION IS THE OPPOSITE OF THE FIGHT-FLIGHT RESPONSE

Meditation is a response of the nervous system. Scientists call it the "Relaxation Response" and, not only is it the opposite of the fight-flight response, but regular meditation prevents the triggering of the fight-flight response and the ravages of hypertension.

Specifically. Meditation has the following effects:

- It decreases the body's oxygen consumption, which reduces metabolism to a point called hypometabolism which is a very restful state that takes a great deal of strain off the body's energy resources.
- It increases the amount of alpha brain waves, which induces the body to relax deeply.
- It decreases the production of blood lactate, thus reducing anxiety.
- It decreases the heart rate.
- It decreases the respiration rate.

Meditation, then, is both a preventative and a remedial technique for dealing with stress. While on this subject, I want to mention three other strategies for dealing with stress, after meditation and goal-setting. If you have two or three of these acts together and you are a regular meditator, you are well on your way to dealing successfully with stress.

MAJOR STRESS REDUCER #3, DIET

The best advice I can think of here is to hire a Nutritionist to help you identify and establish healthy eating habits. Over the years, I have learned that the professionals know more than the informed amateurs and the same is true in the area of nutrition. Nutritionists have told me that food no longer holds the nutrition that it used to 40 years or so ago because the soil doesn't have the same mineral content that it used to. As a result, food supplementation is necessary and here are what Nutritionists tell me are the basic elements of a balanced diet:

- *Food-based enzymes.* Contrary to popular opinion, we are not what we eat, we are what we absorb. Enzymes break down the food that we eat and help us to absorb the nutrients into the blood stream. Today, most of the enzymes have been extracted from vegetables so that they can travel and stay on the grocer's shelf for a profitable period of time. If the enzymes were left in the produce, it would all rot while en route to the retailer.

- *Probiotics.* These are the friendly bacteria that reside in the digestive tract. Their job is to fight the "bad" bacteria and parasites that congregate in the tract as well as assist the nutrients to pass through the intestinal wall. They also work to move the waste through the small intestine and bowel. Without eating extra bacteria such as acidophilus and bifidus, we would lose the war that is being constantly waged in the digestive track and waste would pile up, stretching the walls of the intestine. Eventually toxins would leak through the intestinal wall, they would pollute the blood stream and contaminate every cell of the body, leading ultimately to degenerative disease.

- *Food-Based Vitamins.* Vitamins are essential if the body is to function properly. They regulate metabolism and facilitate the extraction of energy from food.
- *Food-Based Minerals.* Minerals are also essential if the body is to function properly. They are necessary for the healthy make up of bodily fluids, bone, blood and nerves. There are two groups of minerals: Bulk minerals and trace minerals. Bulk minerals include calcium, magnesium, sodium, potassium and phosphorus. Trace minerals are needed in micro amounts and include zinc, iron, copper, manganese, chromium, selenium and iodine.
- *Amino Acids.* Amino acids are the chemical building blocks that make up proteins. Proteins are essential for the creation, growth and maintenance of muscle, bone, organs, tendons, ligaments, nails, hair and most body fluids.
- *Food-based Anti-Oxidants.* Our bodies naturally produce free radicals, which are atoms that contain unpaired electrons. These free electrons can attach to other molecules and drastically alter their makeup and function. Anti-oxidants are a group of vitamins, minerals and enzymes that work to prevent the body from forming free radicals. Examples include: Vitamin A, Vitamin C, Vitamin E, Gamma-Linoleic Acid, L-Cysteine, L-Glutathione, Selenium and Superoxide Dismutase.
- *Dietary Fibre.* Refining processes have removed much of the natural fibre from our foods and, as a result, colon cancer,

constipation, hemorrhoids and obesity are on the rise. Popular forms of fiber include: bran, cellulose, gums, hemi-cellulose, lignin, mucilages and pectin.

- *Coenzyme Q_{10}*. Besides being a very powerful antioxidant, Q_{10} increases the effectiveness of the immune system, slows down the aging process and is used in the treatment of heart disease and hypertension. It is naturally produced by the body but stores start to deplete around age 35 or so and it needs to be supplemented.

MAJOR STRESS REDUCER #4, AEROBIC EXERCISE

The next stress reducing strategy is to engage in aerobic exercise. When experiencing the fight-flight response and we do not either fight or run, the chemicals emitted by the response pool in the body and begin to cause trouble such as clogging of the arteries. Fighting, running or some form of aerobic exercise will dissipate this pooling of the chemicals.

For such exercise to be effective, it should be engaged in at least three times per week, sustained for a minimum of 20 minutes and should get the heart pumping to about 75% of its maximum rate.

For most of us, exercise is a drag and, when it is, we just don't keep it up. The trick is to find an aerobic activity that we really enjoy and can "get into." I have somehow convinced myself that running is a sport and weekend 10-Ks have reinforced this idea. For others, they have to find a game where they chase a ball or puck, whack projectiles across a net, engage in some form of dance or belong to a team. These can all provide valid forms of aerobic exercise and, if we don't find one that we really enjoy, the chances are slim that we will persist and maintain a decent level of aerobic fitness.

MAJOR STRESS REDUCER #5, BE A PLEASURE-SEEKER

The final stress reducing strategy is to regularly engage in activities that bring us pleasure. Be a pleasure-seeker and get your mind totally immersed in something that removes you from the day-to-day activities that bring on the stress. Get involved in a hobby or a sport that will totally engage your attention.

The candidates are limitless. Gardeners will attest to the therapeutic value of their activity as will, painters, wood workers, stamp collectors, bird watchers, hikers, motorcycle enthusiasts, Elvis fans, amateur poets, wine makers, etc.

SUMMARY

The five best stress-reducing strategies that I have found are:
- daily meditation
- goal-setting
- an intelligent diet
- aerobic exercise
- being a pleasure-seeker

For any number of reasons, most of us won't or cannot engage in all five. If we could take the time, however, I'm convinced that we would be healthier, live longer, look younger and enjoy life more. Perhaps, the best we can do is to be aware of these five areas and, given our various constraints and circumstances, make little advances on any or all of them that we can.

A GUIDED MEDITATION

Many people enjoy and/or prefer a guided meditation where another person's voice becomes the mantra. Usually, the person's voice follows a script and leads the meditator(s) through a scenario that involves visualization, affirmations and/or deep relaxation. The following is such a guided meditation where the script can be spoken by another person, you can record it and play it back on a tape recorder or you can just think it to yourself. Here is the script:

> *"Sit in a comfortable position, eyes closed and back straight. Just empty your mind and take three deep breaths, relaxing more deeply with each exhalation.*
>
> *Now, imagine that about three feet above your head there is a round ball of shimmering white light. This light is a friendly light and it is pulsating with warmth and healing energy.*

*The light descents to a point about two or three inches above
your head where you can begin to feel its warmth. It is a
pleasant feeling and you know that this warmth brings with
it a feeling of deep relaxation and healing.*

*The light now descends to sit upon the crown of your head where
it feels very comfortable and you can begin to feel a sense of deep
relaxation. You can feel the light draw up the tension from your
scalp and replace it with peace and tranquility.*

*The light now begins to slowly melt and pour gently down the
sides, front and back of your head. As it does, you can feel the
tension go out of your scalp and be replaced by a sense of deep
relaxation. You can feel your forehead give up its tension; you
can feel the same around your eyes and ears. As the tension
leaves, it is replaced by a feeling of deep relaxation, peace and
tranquility.*

*The light now travels downward, over your ears and eyes to your
mouth and over your jaw. You can feel the tension and anxiety
leave the nerves of your jaw line, you can feel your mouth relax
very deeply and you can feel a deeper sense of peace and tranquility.*

*The light now flows over your neck. You can feel the muscles in
the back and sides of your neck give up their tension, and you
can feel your throat relaxing very deeply.*

After your neck is in a state of deep relaxation, the light settles onto your shoulders and you can fee it absorb the tension and anxiety that has been accumulating in the large muscles of this area. These muscles become very deeply relaxed, giving up all of their tension.

The light now begins to travel down your arms. You can feel its warmth and you can feel the biceps and triceps giving up their tension and becoming heavy with the deep relaxation that is setting in. Similarly, as the light moves over your elbows, you can feel these joints relax very deeply.

As the light flows slowly and gently over your forearms, they become very heavy with the deep relaxation that is setting in. The light flows over your wrists, replacing all the tension with deep relaxation, peace and tranquility.

The light now travels over your hands and along your fingers to the ends of your fingernails. As it does so, it absorbs all of the tension and replaces it with deep, deep relaxation. You can now feel your entire arms deeply relaxed, free of all tension and anxiety.

The light sitting on your shoulders begins to slowly pour down your back and chest. You can feel the large muscles of your upper back give up all of their tension and you can feel the same sensations in the large muscles of your chest. As the light continues downward, it flows over your stomach and abdomen and over your sides and lower back.

Taking a moment, you can enjoy the sensation of all the tension and pressure leaving to be replaced by the deep relaxation and peacefulness of the light.

Your entire upper body is now encased in the light and it feels exceptionally comfortable, peaceful and deeply relaxed.

The light continues its journey downward and you can feel it flowing over your hips and upper legs. As it covers these large muscles, you can feel them give up all of their tension and anxiety as the deep relaxation sets in.

The light flows over the knees drawing all of the tension from these large joints. You can feel the deep relaxation setting in as all of the tension and anxiety are drawn into the light.

The downward journey continues over your calves and shins. You can feel these muscles tingle and give up their tension and you can feel the ankle joints relax very deeply as the light flows over them as well.

The light now travels over your feet; it covers your toes and flows over the sides of your feet to touch the floor. You can feel your feet relax very deeply as the light draws out all the tension and anxiety.

You are now totally encased in this white, shimmering, healing light. You can feel sensations in your body where the light is working. As well, if you have areas of your body that are injured or otherwise hurting, imagine the light going to these areas and bringing its healing, rejuvenating power.

Just take a few moments now to put your attention on various areas of your body and feel the light doing its work.

Now, the light begins to lift off the floor and come up over the sides of you feet as well as the toes, heels and tops of your feet leaving them totally relaxed and revitalized.

The light rises up over your ankles and you can feel the deep relaxation that has settled into these joints. It begins up your shins and calves and you can feel a tingling sensation, letting you know that these muscles are totally relaxed and rejuvenated.

The light rises up over your knees and you can feel the absence of all tension and the effects of the deep relaxation.

You can feel the light rising up your upper legs leaving the large muscles of the fronts, sides and backs fully relaxed and surprisingly powerful. The light rises further up over your hips and lower abdomen to your waist. Your lower body is now fully relaxed and totally revitalized.

The light now continues its upward journey, over your lower back and your stomach. It rises up your sides and now over your upper back and chest, leaving your entire torso deeply relaxed and refreshingly energized. The light lifts off your fingers and travels up your hands to your wrists. You can feel the deep relaxation in your hands.

The light travels over your wrists and you can feel the sensation of relaxation and revitalization in these joints. It moves up your forearms leaving these muscles heavy with the deep relaxation. And, it travels up your upper arms to your shoulders. You can feel both arms deeply relaxed, rejuvenated and powerful.

The light now rises up off your shoulders leaving the muscles and nerves in a state of deep relaxation and well-being. It travels up your neck and you can feel the muscles in the back of your neck give up the last of their tension.

As the light rises up the sides of your head, you can feel that all of the tension and stress has left the nerves of your jaw line and the areas around your mouth, ears and eyes.

Finally, the light is rising up the upper portion of your head removing the last vestiges of stress and tension from your scalp.

The light finally resumes its round shape and sits on the crown of your head shimmering and pulsating with healing restorative energy.

As the light sits there, you know at the deepest level of your being that this light has worked its magic in providing deep relaxation to your entire body. It has drawn out all of the stress, tension and anxiety and has replaced it with peace, tranquility and deep, deep relaxation. This is a healing light and it is your friend.

Now, as the light begins to slowly lift off your head, you experience a sense of gratitude for its gifts and you feel contentment in knowing that this light will return to do its work any time you wish. All you have to do to summon it is to imagine it sitting above you head ready to do you bidding and it will be there. And, as you are pleased to know this, the ball of light now rises up more quickly, moves off into the distance, and disappears."

This is a progressive relaxation exercise and it is an excellent example of visualization. I have used this guided meditation many times and have had people report that they have felt the warmth from the imaginary light, some have reported that pain went away and all have reported feeling refreshed, relaxed and a greater sense of well-being.

A SEMI-GUIDED MEDITATION

Sometimes, you can create a partially guided meditation and let your imagination fill in the rest. This is interesting to do in a group, as the members will all report different experiences,

some quite fascinating. Here's an example of how it can work:
Go into a meditative state for about eight to ten minutes. When
you (or the group) are comfortably meditating, the guide's voice
says:

*"You are standing alone on a country road. It can be one with
which you are familiar or one that you have never seen before.
You begin to walk along this road and, as you do, you notice
what a perfect day it is. You notice the warm, bright sun and the
blue, cloudless sky. You can feel the sun's warmth on your body.
You can hear birds singing and you can smell the fresh, moist
blossoms. You can hear the wind in the trees and you can hear
the sound of splashing water from the brook that runs parallel to
the road. The day is perfect and you are fully in tune with it.*

*As you proceed along the road, you are perfectly at peace,
enjoying the sights, the sounds and the country smells. You
notice, up ahead, that the road turns a corner and you cannot
see where it leads from there. Something tells you, however, that
around the corner is a scene that is even more beautiful than the
one you have been experiencing. You don't know what it is but
you have a very strong feeling that what you are about to
encounter will be wonderful.*

*As you approach the turn in the road, you are getting excited
because you know deeply that you are about to experience something spectacular. You are now about ten paces from the turn*

*and you can hardly wait to get there. You are now five paces
away, four, three, two, one — you turn the corner. What you see
before you is yours to explore and enjoy. Go to it."*

It is fun to do this in a group and then let each member of the
group report their experience. I've heard of people suddenly
skiing down great mountains, encountering talking animals,
asking questions to gurus and hiking into beautiful valleys. The
experiences are as varied as are individuals' imaginations.

5

APPLICATIONS

We see metaphysical principles and applications at work every day. Every moment of our existence is something that we create. We do this so easily and naturally that we are not aware that we are doing it.

In this section, I have introduced five subjects, which, for most of us, are areas of metaphysical application that are not so natural or ordinary. In exploring and playing with these areas, we can become more skilful with each of them and we will indubitably encounter more ways to enjoy our pursuit of self-discovery.

1. PAST LIFE REGRESSION

THERE REALLY ARE NO PAST LIVES.

Remember, that from the perspective of the higher self, all of our lives are happening simultaneously. It is only from our earthly perspective that we have past and future lives.

We get short glimpses of other lives in our dreams and in such instances as déjà vu. These are usually quite fuzzy and confusing, and, typically, they don't give us as much information about a particular life as they do about a moment in a life. As such, they are usually not very meaningful or helpful.

One of the ways to get a fuller picture of a past life is through past life regression where a facilitator regresses a subject. There are a number of methods for regressing someone, some more effective than others. Here is one that I find works quite well.

PREPARE CAREFULLY.

First, the subject should understand that throughout the regression session, he/she is in full control. This is not an exercise where the facilitator imposes his/her will on the subject. The subject will not do or say anything that he/she will not want to.

Before the session begins, both parties should use the washroom and the subject should remove any contact lenses and false eyelashes. It is a good idea to have a box of facial tissues handy, as there could be some tears that need wiping.

The facilitator may want to take some notes, so, a pen and paper should be at hand and a good quality tape recorder should be set up to capture the entire session. The subject lies comfortably on a sofa, a massage table, a bed or upon a comfortable floor mat. The facilitator usually sits in a chair fairly near to the subject's head where the conversation can be easily heard and where the facilitator can see the subject's eyes. The room's lights are dimmed and the subject may have a light blanket pulled up near to the chin.

IT IS IMPORTANT THAT THE SUBJECT BE RELAXED.

Before beginning a regression session, it is important to ensure that the subject is relaxed. This is done by spending some time going through a progressive relaxation routine, suggesting that each part of the body relax, starting with the toes and working upward towards the head. Be sure to take your time and deliver the suggestions slowly and clearly, giving the subject plenty of time to focus on the parts of the body that you are speaking about. This is done with the subject's eyes closed. You can use your own words or you can use the following script:

"Close your eyes and allow yourself to clear your mind and fall into a mellow, relaxed mood. Feel your body become heavy with a sense of deep, deep relaxation. Feel the troubles of the day drift

away as you take this time out to enjoy a period of care-free, deep relaxation.

First, your feet are letting go of all their tension and stress. You can feel your toes relax very deeply. You can feel the tension lift out of the tops of your feet, you can feel your arches letting go of their tension and you can sense the relaxation settling into your heals. Take a moment and focus your mind on how relaxed and free of tension your feet have become.

Next, put your attention on your ankles. Feel these joints give up their tension and fall into a state of deep, deep relaxation. Feel the sense of deep relaxation travel up your lower legs, taking all of the stress and tension out of your shins and calf muscles. Feel these muscles fall into this state of deep, deep relaxation and loose all of their tension, stress and anxiety.

Now, you can feel this state of relaxation settling into your knees. These large joints house so much stress and tension, and you can feel all of this tension leaving only to be replaced by the very pleasant sensations of the deep relaxation.

The state of deep relaxation travels further upward as it enters your upper legs where you feel the large muscles of your thighs giving up all of their stress and tension and take on this state of deep, deep relaxation. You can feel it in the large quadriceps in the front and outside of your upper legs. You can feel it in the large hamstring muscles in the back of your legs. Both of your legs are now totally relaxed from the soles of your feet to the tops of your thighs. Just take a moment and focus your attention on your legs. Feel the heaviness that has set in with the very deep relaxation and the total release of all tension, stress and anxiety.

The relaxation, in its upward travel, fills your hips and lower torso. You can feel the large muscles of your hips giving up all of their tension and stress and you can feel the deep, deep relaxation setting in. You can feel this sense of relaxation enter your lower back as any tension or pain shrinks and disappears.

The large muscles of your back, sides and abdomen release their tension and begin to relax very deeply. You can feel the tension leaving and the relaxation penetrate and bring a sense of relief and peacefulness.

You can feel your arms give up their tension. First, the larger muscles of the upper arms begin to relax. Your triceps and biceps begin to get heavier as they relax and give up their tension and stress. Next, the forearms begin to get heavier as they too relax and their tension evaporates. The sense of relaxation moves into your wrists and, finally, into your hands where each of your fingers becomes heavy with the deep, deep relaxation, free of all tension. Your arms are now fully relaxed, they are very heavy and they are free of all tension, stress and anxiety.

Next, your shoulders begin to relax. The large muscles at the tops of your shoulders give up their tension and stress, and you can

*feel the relaxation settling in, giving you a feeling of freedom
from tension and stress.*

*The muscles of your neck begin to release their tension and become
very deeply relaxed. You can feel the relaxation taking over the
back of your neck, the sides and the area of your throat. You can
feel the tension leaving the large nerve centre around your jawline.
You can feel the area around your mouth relax very deeply and
you can feel all of the tension and stress leave your facial muscles
and in particular, the areas around your eyes and ears.*

*You can now feel your entire scalp releasing its tension and you
can enjoy the feeling of the deep, deep relaxation setting into your
entire head.*

*Take a moment now and just notice how heavy your entire body
feels because it is so totally relaxed and free of tension and stress.
Put your attention on your feet, your lower legs, your knees, your
upper legs, and the area around your hips and lower back. Feel
the large muscles of your upper back and torso. Feel the heaviness in your arms giving witness to the very deep relaxation that
has settled in. Put your attention on the muscles of your shoulders
and feel the relaxed condition of your neck, face and entire scalp."*

When going through a routine such as this, don't be afraid of
repeating some of the same phrases. This will actually reinforce
your suggestions making them more comfortable for the subject
and, consequently, more effective.

When you are working with a subject who has been through progressive relaxation routines before, and you judge that it is appropriate, you may abbreviate the procedure by not going into as much detail. Some people can relax deeply almost instantly, but it is still a good idea to suggest that they relax the major body parts, starting with the toes and progressing to the head

Once you believe that the subject is deeply relaxed, ask the subject how he/she feels. If they are comfortable and relaxed, it is time to move on. If not, ask them what you can do to make them more comfortable and then, within reason, accommodate their wishes. Once they are settled, comfortable and relaxed, move forward. In some rare instances, you may have a subject who just cannot get comfortable. If this is the case, it is probably wise to abort the effort because they don't appear ready and this is not something that you want to force.

Before starting the actual regression, it is important to have the subject relax even more deeply. You can do this by counting them down. Again, you can follow a script or use your own words. Here is a script that you might follow:

"To help you relax even more deeply, I am going to count from ten to zero. By the time I reach zero, your body will be in a state of very deep relaxation. While your body is in this very deep state, your mind will be fully alert, clear and you will be easily able to communicate with me. You will be in complete control of this entire exercise. You will hear my voice clearly and you will be easily able to answer my questions and tell me about your experiences and feelings.

Ten, nine, eight... with each count you are going deeper and deeper into a state of peaceful relaxation. Seven, six, five...deeper yet and more and more relaxed. You can feel your entire body sinking ever deeper. Four, three, two... you are in a most comfortable and peaceful state of deep rest. one, zero... Your body is now totally relaxed and yet your mind is clear and alert. You are able to easily hear me and you can easily speak with me, answering my questions and letting me know your impressions and feelings."

FIRST, RECALL SOME PLEASANT CHILDHOOD EXPERIENCES.

A good number of subjects have some degree of apprehension or reluctance about being regressed. Many have doubts that it can be done or else feel that they will somehow fail to be successful. To get the ball rolling and to test these waters, it is helpful to ask the subject to recall some pleasant childhood experiences. You might, for example, pursue a script like the following:

"Pick a time in your childhood when you were generally quite happy and imagine that you are standing in front of the home you lived in at that time. See yourself as you were then and notice how you feel. Look at the home and notice some of its features. Notice the height of the structure, its colour and shape. Observe some of its surroundings such as any trees, gardens or paved areas. Describe it to me."

Here, let the subject speak and, as you feel it is appropriate, ask some simple questions about the house or apartment building. Ask about the surroundings, what kind of day it is, who lived here with them, can they hear birds singing, can they smell blossoms, etc.

Next, ask the subject to recall and describe an experience around that time that was a happy occasion. Ask them to see themselves as they were then and to feel the feelings that they had at that time. Ask for details and ask them to describe their feelings.

Now, ask the subject to go back in time to very early childhood, to their first childhood memory. Ask them, again, to see themselves as they were then and to feel the feelings that they had then. Ask them to describe this memory to you. Ask for details and the associated feelings. What the subject tells you will suggest questions that you may ask. Let your intuition and judgement guide you as you probe to get the full picture.

If the subject reports that he/she is not able to recall an early childhood memory, ask for the reason why. Again, be guided by your intuition and best judgement as to how you respond to their answer. Chances are that, if they tell you what is blocking their memory, they will either give you clues or a clear way to overcome the blockage.

START THE ACTUAL REGRESSION.

Here, you want to suggest a scenario that will elicit past life memories. There is a variety of ways to do this. The following is one routine that I find simple and effective. I'll suggest a few others at the end of this section.

Again, you can follow the routine verbatim or you can use your own words to follow the basic outline. Ideally, keep your words simple and let the subject supply his/her own interpretations and reactions.

"I would like you to imagine that you are standing on a country road. It may be a road that you are familiar with, or not, it doesn't matter. The time is somewhere around mid-day, the weather is bright and sunny and the temperature is pleasantly warm. As you look around, you see tall trees, fields with a variety of grasses and bright wild flowers. Off in the distance, you can see the outline of hills.

When you listen, you can hear birds singing and the sounds of crickets and other insects. As you breath in, you enjoy the various scents from the wild flowers and from the trees. All of your senses are pleasantly stimulated and you feel energetic and totally at peace. This is a perfect day and you are in a perfect setting.

You now begin to walk along this road and, as you do so, you are happy to take in all of the sights, sounds and scents as you go. You are thoroughly enjoying the day and yourself. You are also enjoying the exercise of walking. There is energy in your stride and, although you are in no particular hurry, you are nevertheless moving quite briskly, while taking in all of your surroundings.

You look up ahead and notice that the road takes a turn to the right. You don't know what is around this turn but you have the distinct feeling that it will be something very pleasant. Your pace picks up a little with a sense of quiet excitement and you approach the turn feeling that you are about to have a most exciting and beneficial experience.

You now turn the corner and you see a magnificent valley spread out before you. The road continues down into the valley and you can see that it ends at a river. At the river's edge is a bridge that will take you over the river. The river is not very wide, perhaps a hundred feet or so, but you cannot see the other side because there is a mist that covers the river and it only allows you to see about half way across. Even though you cannot see to the other side of the river, you feel excited about crossing the bridge because you can feel that something good awaits you on the other side.

You continue to walk down the road until you come to the bridge. You like this bridge. It's made of strong wood, it's very solid and you feel safe about walking on this bridge. You step onto the bridge, it feels solid under your feet and it slopes gently upward to the centre. You can't see the other side because the mist is too thick but you like the idea of getting there. So, with this pleasant feeling of anticipation, you begin to walk along the bridge. As you move forward, the mist begins to clear in front of you so that you can see further. When you get to the half-way point, you begin to realize that, when you get to the other side of the river, you will be in a past life. This idea excites you because you realize that this is a past life in which you were very happy and really enjoyed the things that you experienced.

As you start downward, you have about twenty paces to go before you reach the other side. You are feeling good about this, the mist is beginning to clear and you are now able to see an outline of the shore. As you move towards the end of the bridge, you now have about ten paces left. You are walking easily and comfortably. Five paces to go, four, three, two, one. You step off the bridge and you are now in that past lifetime."

BEGIN WITH OPEN-ENDED QUESTIONS.

At this point, you begin to ask questions and, it is usually best to start with open-ended questions. You might, for example, start with: *"Describe for me what you see around you."* As you begin to get information, pursue it with follow-up questions. For example, the subject might tell you that she sees a party going on. You might follow with: *"A party. Tell me what's happening."* (Still leaving it quite open-ended). She might say something like: *"Everyone is dancing."* You might ask: *"What else?"*

FOLLOW WITH MORE SPECIFIC PROBES.

You can continue to ask about this event and, as the dialogue continues, your questions can get more pointed. For example:

Subject: *"There are musicians playing music and there are lots of food and things to drink."*

You: *"What sort of occasion is this?"*

Subject: *"It's my wedding."*

You: *"How are you feeling?"*

Subject: *"I'm feeling very happy and I'm enjoying every minute."*

You: *"Describe for me what you are wearing."*

Subject: *"I have a beautiful grass skirt and I'm wearing a bright necklace made of tropical flowers, orchids, I think. There are flowers in my hair and bracelets and anklets made of colourful seashells and tiny bones."*

You: *"What is your name?"*

Subject: *"Taralua."*

You: *Taralua* (And you would use her name from that life), *how old are you?*

Subject: *"I'm seventeen."*

COUNT THE SUBJECT FORWARD OR BACKWARD IN TIME.

When you feel that you have exhausted a particular event or scene, you can move the subject to another time period in that same life. You can do this by counting them either forward of backward in time. For example, you might say:

> *"Taralua, I'm going to count to three and, by the time I say three, you will be back at the time of your twelfth birthday, where you will be able to describe for me what is happening around you One, two, three. You are now at your twelfth birthday, what is going on around you?*

> *Alternatively, you might say: "Taralua, I'm going to count to three and, by the time I say three, you will be twenty-five years old. You will know where you are and you will be able to describe the things that are going on around you. One, two, three. You are now twenty-five. What is happening around you?*

VISIT THE DEATH SCENE.

Of course, it could happen that Taralua never lived to be twenty-five and, when you ask her to go to that age, she will either be silent or she may tell you that she never lived to be twenty-five. If she is silent or seems stalled, ask her what the problem is or why she isn't at age twenty-five. Chances are she will tell you. Whether she does or not, I suggest that you count to three and take her to the time of her death and ask her to describe the circumstances of that event.

WHEN THE GOING GETS TOUGH, YOU HAVE THREE OPTIONS.

Usually, a subject will be quite objective about their death and not get particularly emotional. On the other hand, a little weeping or expressions of joy, anger or sadness are not uncommon. On occasion, the event of one's death or other distressing events may involve circumstances that are very difficult for the subject to relive. In such instances, you have three options:

One, you can have the subject stay with the event and experience all of the thoughts and feelings. You might say something like:

"Although this may be difficult for you, stay with the feelings. Feel them fully, knowing that this is from the past and cannot hurt you now. Describe how you feel."

Two, you can have the subject become the observer of the event and not experience the thoughts and feelings directly. You could say something like:

"I will count to three and when I say three, you will have removed yourself from your body, you will be floating above the scene and you will be looking down upon it, just being the observer. You will be perfectly safe and what you see will not

*upset you. One, two, three. You are now out of your body,
looking down upon this scene. What do you see now? How do
you feel?"*

Three, you can remove the subject from the scene altogether by
saying something like:

*"OK, I am going to count to three and when I say three, you
will leave this period of time and move on to a happy time in
this same life. One, two, three. Describe this time for me."*

The easiest way to decide which course to follow is to simply ask
the subject if he/she thinks that the present situation should be
experienced. Usually they will say yes and you just stay with the
first option. If the subject appears too distressed to stay with the
event, try removing them from their body and have them
become the observer. The third option is available if you feel
conditions are too upsetting to persist.

IT IS BEST TO FACE A DISTURBING EVENT.

If a disturbing event arouses a good deal of emotion and anxiety,
it is valid to face the event to understand it and to learn from it
but there is a balance to achieve between this and prolonging the
negative experience unduly. Once the subject has confronted and
relived such an event, you can suggest that he/she has visited it
long enough, that it is time to move on and that the subject is

once again feeling relaxed and at peace. You can then count them on to a happier time in that same life.

A typical regression session will visit one or two satisfying highlights in a particular past life, perhaps one or two troubling or problematic events and the time of one's death. Additionally, an important base to touch before ending the session is a visit to the past life that is resonating the most in the present life.

VISIT THE LIFE THAT RESONATES MOST TODAY.

Each life has an influence on all of an individual's other lives but, usually, one or a small number of past lives stand out from the others by having particular impact. Ask the subject to identify a life that has a strong influence today. The impact of this life may stem from a single event such as a murder, an act of great self-sacrifice or an exceptional achievement. On the other hand, the life's significance may be the result of the whole life or a major portion of it, e.g. a life of being dominated, one of being in someone's debt, or one that had a special long term relationship.

To visit this life, you might suggest something like the following:

> "At this point, I am going to count to three and when I say three, you will be in the lifetime that has the greatest significance in your current life and you will be able to witness the events or the circumstances that give this lifetime its significance for your present life. One, two, three... describe what you see now."

Before leaving this life, make sure the subject has discovered the events or circumstances that are resonating in their present life and that they have identified the lessons that they may carry into the present. You might say something like:

> *"Now that you have visited this life and have seen the events or circumstances that have created a strong influence in your present life, describe exactly what the significance of this life is for your present life and describe any lessons that you may have learned from this experience."*

CONSIDER UNDERTAKING SOME ACTION OR NEW BEHAVIOUR.

At this point, you have the opportunity of ensuring that the subject will undertake some new, positive action in light of this new knowledge. You might pursue a line such as:

> *"Jane, now that you understand the significance of this past live, what do you think an appropriate new behaviour might be?"*

If Jane identifies a new behaviour or action, reinforce it by telling her that this is a good idea and, now that she understands the significance of her new knowledge, she understands why she should undertake the new behaviour or action, and that she will find it easy to do.

To illustrate this idea, consider the example of the overweight woman who discovered in a past life that she was very beautiful and that, as a wartime captive, she was singled out for abuse because of her beauty. In her current life, she constantly ate in order to become fat and unattractive because, at an unconscious level, she did not want to be beautiful again and risk a repeat of the abuse. Upon visiting the past life in which she was abused, she quickly realized that overeating today was no longer relevant. With this realization, she changed her eating habits and achieved a normal weight.

Once the subject identifies an action or behaviour to undertake, suggest that he/she will be able to recall the events or circumstances from that life that are resonating today, that they will fully understand the significance of these events or circumstances in their present life and that they will be easily able to undertake any new and appropriate actions or behaviours. You might say:

> *"After we end this session, you will be able to recall all of the events and circumstances that are resonating in your present life today, you will fully understand their significance and you will be easily able to begin the new habit of..."*

After visiting the life that resonates the most in the present life, it is nearing time to end the session. Before doing so, it is a good idea to ask the subject if he/she would like to end the session now or if there is anything further that they would like to explore in this session. You will find that the subject has either had enough for now or that he/she might wish to explore other events in the current lifetime or possibly move on to another life. Take your cue from the subject and either count them on or end the session. Typically, a session would last for about one hour. If the subject is easily and quickly regressed, it could be shorter.

At this point in the session, the subject is either deeply relaxed or you can quickly get them that way by suggesting that they are in a peaceful, relaxed state. In such a state, they are highly suggestible and this is an ideal time to do any of the following three things.

TAKE THE OPPORTUNITY TO MAKE SOME POSITIVE SUGGESTIONS.

First, you can make positive suggestions impacting their health. For example, you might suggest that the immune system be strengthened or that relief be brought to any injuries or ailments.

Second, you have the opportunity of assisting the subject to reduce or eliminate any negative habits that he/she may wish to. Your best bet for doing this is to have the subject visualize or imagine what it would be like to live without the habit, e.g. smoking, over-eating, etc. Once they see themselves in this more positive state, have them describe how it feels. Normally, they will articulate very positive feelings. Ask them if this is the way they would prefer to be. Chances are they will say yes. You can then suggest that all they have to do is strongly resolve that they will undertake this new behaviour for their higher good and ask them if they will. When they say yes, you can reinforce their resolve by congratulating them and affirming that, indeed, their new behaviour will replace the former negative one.

Third, you have the opportunity of suggesting that the events and circumstances that were experienced in the current session will be recalled and their meanings understood. You might tell them something like: *"Jane, before we leave this session, you will recall the events that we visited and you will understand their significance for your current life."* Failure to do this will result in the memories fading quickly and they will likely not be recalled unless you take the subject through another session.

BRING THE SESSION TO AN END.

To bring the regression session to an end, you can tell the subject something like:

> *"We will now end the session. I will count forward from one to ten and by the time I reach ten, you will be fully awake, feeling refreshed, energized and at peace. You will recall all that has transpired in this session and you will fully understand its significance for your present life. One, two, three... you are beginning to come back to your present life, feeling very refreshed and peaceful. Four, five, six... you are coming back to your normal waking state. Seven, eight... you will recall perfectly all that has transpired in this session and you will know the significance of the past events that you have visited. Nine, ten... you are now fully awake, feeling refreshed, energized and at peace. Stay lying down and very slowly, open your eyes"*

At this point, give the subject a moment or two to collect himself or herself and to take their time in sitting up.

IT IS IMPORTANT TO DEBRIEF EACH SESSION.

The final activity is to spend a few moments debriefing. Ask the subject how he/she feels about the experience and ask what they feel are the important highlights and lessons. Spending a little time here can elicit additional insights and draw more meaning. It is also not a bad idea to ask the subject to write a summary of what just happened, adding their interpretation of the events and the meanings they feel these events have for their life here and now. Sometimes, additional insights are developed hours and days after the session.

OTHER IMAGES THAT CAN FACILITATE REGRESSION.

In the forgoing session, a bridge was used to lead the subject over time to a past life. I told you earlier that I would outline some other images that can be used. Here are three:

You can suggest that the subject is in a boat, drifting with the current and travelling down a river. There is a mist over the river such that they can only see the river bank if they turn towards the shore. The subject has control of the boat and is guided to turn in to the shore. Each time the subject touches shore, he/she is in a different past life. They are then directed to get out of the boat, stand on the shore and begin to describe what they see. From there, you can lead them through various events as was done before with the bridge scenario.

Second, you can suggest that the subject is walking down a long corridor that has doors on each side. Each door represents an entrance to a past life. The further down the corridor the subject walks, the further back in time he/she is travelling. You can direct the subject to go to a door that represents a happy or a significant lifetime, open the door and describe what lies ahead, much as you might have done using the bridge or the river.

Third, a tunnel is often used where the subject is told that he/she is entering a tunnel that will take them back in time to other lifetimes. You can direct them by counting backwards from twenty, telling them that they will emerge from the tunnel in a previous lifetime. Once they have emerged, you can ask them to describe what they see.

I am sure there are other images that can be used to elicit a past life regression. The forgoing are the ones that I have had some exposure to and I suspect each facilitator will have to experiment to find the most effective one for them and for their subjects. I like the bridge best as its image seems comfortable for nearly everyone. Certainly those with claustrophobia might find the tunnel or the corridor a little too confining while those who cannot swim might balk at drifting down a river where they can't see the shore.

SUMMARY:

Below, I have summarized the forgoing steps in a format that can serve as a guide or checklist for the facilitator. I have printed this out on a single sheet that I use as a list of prompts when I conduct a session. You might find it similarly helpful, either as is or with your own modifications.

- Remind the subject that he/she is in control and can end the session anytime he/she wishes
- Both parties go to the washroom
- Have tissues handy
- Remove contact lenses and false eyelashes
- Have a tape recorder and pen and paper at hand
- Subject lying down with light blanket
- Progressive relaxation from toes to head
- Ensure subject is comfortable
- Reminder that the subject is in complete control and will be able to communicate easily with you
- Count subject down from ten to zero
- Recall pleasant childhood experiences
  - Standing in front of home
  - A childhood experience
  - Earliest childhood experience they can recall
- Regression technique, e.g. the bridge
  - Country road
  - The turn in the road
  - Over the bridge

- What do you see?
  - Probes
- Counting forward and back, 1-2-3
- Death scene
- Life resonating the most today
  - Identify lesson(s) and/or new behaviour
- End the session
  - Suggestions Re: Health
  - Suggestions Re: Habits
  - Suggestions Re: recall and meaning
- Count out from one to ten
- Debrief
  - Record highlights and meanings
- Discuss feelings, lessons, new habits, etc.

2. SEEING AURAS

How many bodies do you have? Most people would regard this as a rather silly question because everyone knows that we were all issued just one. In fact, we have five. The physical one that we all know about is the densest and most apparent, but there are four others.

Ranging from the most dense (slowest vibrational frequency) to the least (highest frequency), our five bodies are:

- The physical body
- The ethereal body
- The emotional or astral body

- The mental body
- The spiritual or causative body.

Each of these bodies is an energy field that has its own unique range of possible vibration frequencies. As an individual grows and develops, the frequency of each of these bodies rises towards the upper end of its respective range. As well, there is not a hard line or border separating these bodies from each other, instead, they blend together.

The ethereal body maintains the shape of the physical body and exists approximately two inches around it. The ethereal body dies with the physical body (a few days after, actually) while the astral, mental and spiritual bodies do not die and reunite with the individual at the time of each incarnation.

The ethereal body has two main functions. First, it acts as a protective shield around the physical body, preventing germs, viruses and bacteria from invading it. Second, it acts as a conduit for information flow between the physical body and the emotional, mental and spiritual bodies.

In the first case, the ethereal body protects the physical body from all external attacks of disease and illness. In effect, we cannot get sick from external causes. However, when our thoughts and emotions are negative or if we engage in undermining behaviours, like poor diet or harmful habits, we weaken the energy flow of the ethereal body and allow germs and other external assaults to penetrate and compromise the good health of the physical body.

That's how we get sickness and disease, they are internally caused, not externally.

In the case of conducting the flow of information, the ethereal body transfers the information received from the senses, from the physical body to the astral and mental bodies. As well, it transfers information from the higher frequency bodies to the physical body. When the ethereal body is weakened, the flow of this information is compromised and the individual will not only risk illness but will appear to be mentally and emotionally slower.

The astral or emotional body assumes an oval shape around the physical body and extends outward for as much as a few metres. It is in a constant state of motion and it contains our emotions and character traits. As an individual evolves emotionally and in character, the astral body takes on a shape more like the physical body and its usual cloudy appearance clears to become bright and colourful.

The astral body's colours reflect the state of the feelings, fears, emotions and character traits of the individual. As these change, so do the colours. The more the individual entertains such positive feelings as joy, love, generosity, etc., the more the astral body will become bright and vibrant. Conversely, as our feelings or character become dark and negative, so do this body's colours.

Remember, the astral body is one of the three bodies that don't die with the physical body. As such, it reunites with us each time that we incarnate. In so doing, it brings with it all of the fears, anxieties, worries and unresolved emotions, along with a range of positive emotions, that we have accumulated from all of our past lives. It is in this body that the greater part of our evolution is carried and reflected.

Given the state of our accumulated emotions, feelings and character traits, a corresponding vibration frequency is set up. As these things change, so does the vibration. The more positive these are, the higher the vibration.

It is here that the law of attraction is played out. Contrary to the common myth, it is likes that attract, not opposites. So, if our astral body is carrying a good deal of fear and negativity, it will carry with it an energy vibration that projects into the world and attracts the vibrations of negative people, circumstances and events. Conversely, positive feelings will attract people, circumstances and events that carry positive energy. In this way, our feelings and emotions contribute immeasurably to the creation of the reality in which we find ourselves living.

When we attract a particular reality, that reality is really a mirror of what resides in our unconscious, and of course, it resides there because, to avoid it, we have shoved it there. When we create a negative reality, we are being shown the specific things that we fear and want to avoid. For example, if we are experiencing an aggressive, hostile environment, it is because we have an unconscious fear of aggression and hostility. Attracting/ creating such an environment gives us the opportunity to confront it, learn to deal with it and thus evolve.

As long as we put off dealing with such negativity, we will continue to attract the circumstances and individuals that will unconsciously reinforce exactly what we are trying to avoid consciously, and the negativity will only grow stronger. As well, as the astral body doesn't die, it will bring all of these unresolved, negative and unconscious feelings, etc. into each successive incarnation. This accounts for why people are born with various amounts of "baggage."

On the other hand, as we confront our fears and negative emotions and resolve them, they are replaced with feelings of love and joy. This raises the energy vibration of the astral body, which causes it to radiate vibrant colour and energy, that in turn, attracts a reality of love, good health and happiness.

This is how we attract our own reality. This is how we are the masters and not the victims. This is how we are the creators. It is the enactment of Bashar's third law of the universe: What you put out is what you get back.

The mental body carries our thoughts, ideas and intuitions. It is oval in shape, extends a few metres beyond our astral body and carries vibrational frequencies that are higher than the ethereal and astral bodies.

When one's thoughts are clear and intuitive and when their awareness is highly developed, the energy vibration is faster and the colours are bright and vibrant. When one's thinking is muddled and rather undeveloped, the vibration is slower and the colour is murky.

The main function of the mental body is to receive intuitions and inspirations from the spiritual realm/body and process this input through the mind so that such ideas and principles can be applied effectively to everyday living at the physical level.

The other thing it does is gather information from the physical body, perceptions and sensations, which are transmitted by the ethereal body through the emotional/astral body. As they pass through the astral body, this information is transformed into feelings and emotions, which in turn, travel to the mental body where related thoughts are formed.

As I pointed out before, the astral body carries many unresolved emotions. When the mental body picks these up, the individual's thinking becomes muddled and distorted, and the mind's ability to generate practical solutions to everyday affairs is compromised.

The other thing that happens is that, as the astral body's unresolved emotions, worries, anxieties, etc. attract a negative reality, that type of reality is reinforced and strengthened when the mental body generates corresponding thoughts.

Of course, it follows that positive emotions in the astral body are picked up by the mental body and the vibration increases, its colours get brighter, the individual's thinking is clearer and more effective, and the individual experiences a more positive reality.

The spiritual or causative body carries the highest vibrational frequency of all the bodies. In an individual who is not very spiritually aware, this body forms an oval approximately a metre around the physical body. In a highly developed individual, this body can extend for miles and take the shape of a perfectly round sphere. The colours of this body are said to be brilliant and spectacular.

Our spiritual body connects us to the spiritual realm where we are able to receive energy of the highest vibration. This energy flows through our mental, astral and ethereal bodies and helps them to increase their vibrations and realize their fullest potential.

Our spiritual body is our connection to the source of all creation. It connects us with the God force and with every other aspect of All That Is. It is the highest aspect of our self.

I said earlier that our ethereal, astral, mental and spiritual bodies don't die. As long as we are living in a material realm, this is true. However, as we evolve through the non-material, emotional and mental realms, the ethereal, astral and mental bodies drop away and we are left with the truly immortal spiritual body of pure consciousness, which is what we ultimately are. It is in this form that we come back to the integrated source from which we began our adventure in experiencing and exploring, as discussed in chapter one.

So, in summary, we have five bodies: The physical one that we all know and are most aware of. The ethereal body that protects us from disease and transmits information from the higher vibrational bodies to the physical body, and visa versa. The astral body, which carries our feelings and emotions and creates much of our physical reality by projecting our emotional state. Our mental body which receives information from the spiritual plain that it processes for practical application in physical life while translating perceptions from the physical body into thoughts. And, the spiritual body which connects us to God and all that that implies.

Note: I thank Shalila Sharamon and Bodo J. Baginski for their elaborate descriptions of the five bodies as found in their book,

The Chakra Handbook, pages nine through twenty. The forgoing is an abstract of their material.

Now, this section is entitled: "Seeing Auras" and, so far, I haven't written about seeing anything. An aura is the light that is generated by the vibrating energy of our different bodies. The more developed such a body is, the more vibrant and colourful is the aura, and the more likely it is that others will be able to see it. As well, the more developed an individual is, the more likely he/she is able to see the auras of other people.

Nearly everyone can see auras. Most people, however, don't know that they can. It seems that some come by it naturally and report that they have always seen auras. Most of us, however, only see them when someone shows us what to look for. Here are three ways you can learn to see auras.

THREE WAYS TO SEE AURAS.

First, you can do this with a friend. Get into a room with light coloured walls and have your friend stand a foot or so away from one of the walls. The larger the room, the better. Make sure the wall is free of pictures, posters, etc.; you want a plain wall for a backdrop. You stand at the opposite end of the room and face your friend. Your friend may face you, the wall or sideways, it doesn't matter. Now dim the lights. You want the room fairly dark but you want to be able to see your friend. You might have to experiment with the lighting but, usually, having the room quite dark works best.

Now look at your friend's head, focus your gaze on his/her hairline. Let your eyes stare without blinking. They will get a little dry and will seem to come in and out of focus. Just relax and continue to stare. Now, notice about an inch or so around their head, there is a fairly bright light. Sometimes you can see, out of your periphery, that this light is all around their entire body, which it is.

Next, continue staring at the head but raise your gaze to about three to five inches above it. Here, you will see a fainter light and, again, from your periphery, without staring directly at it, you should be able to see this light all around the head. Sometimes, you will notice that this light shifts a little so that you see more or less of it at one side of the head, and sometimes, you will notice that the light rises to a conical or rounded point above the head.

The second way that you can see auras is to be vigilant for situations where you might be in an audience where there is a speaker or a cast of actors in front of you on a stage. If the lighting is somewhat dimmed, you can pick one of the people on the stage and adopt your, glassy-eyed stare and direct it to the top of their head. Quite often you can spot the auras of all the individuals on a stage and you will see them move around quite a bit. It seems that people who are speaking or performing on stage have their energy elevated and that their auras are not at all difficult to see.

The third way that you can see auras is to get into a dimly lit room with a large mirror. Again, with your dry, glassy-eyed stare, stare into the mirror and focus your attention on the reflection of the top of your own head. In the same way as you did with your friend, gaze until you see the tight, rather bright light that is close to your body and then direct your gaze to the area a few inches above the head. You should have just as much success doing this with your reflection as you did with your friend.

Over time, if you regularly attempt these exercises, you will become more adept at seeing auras. Most people get some results immediately. Some people see colours in the auras immediately. For most of us, seeing colour comes with practice and seems to happen only once in a while. Sometimes when you see colour it is the aura of a fairly evolved individual. The first time that I saw colour in an aura, it was a bright gold light emanating out of the front of an individual's face when she turned sideways. I knew this individual and knew that she was a highly psychic trance channeller.

Once you achieve some success in seeing auras, look for opportunities regularly. Once, I was sitting in a darkened room staring at my hands. They literally were surrounded in light. Sometimes, outside, you can stare at a bush or tree and see an aura surrounding them. All life has auras. Look for them and, in time, with practice and patience, you will be quite surprised at what you discover. Enjoy.

3. THE OUIJA BOARD

Jane Roberts was the best selling author who channelled Seth. If you are not aware of the Seth books, check them out at any bookstore and you will get a considerable education in metaphysics. Jane was a poet and author in her own rite but she really became famous when she began publishing the Seth books. I don't know how many there are but I have ten and I know there are more that I've yet to read, although, I'm quite happy not to until I've re-read some of the ones that I enjoyed so much the first time through.

Jane Roberts and her husband, Robert F. Butts Jr. started communicating with Seth trough an ouija board. This is a very cumbersome way to communicate, as you have to go letter by letter until you have a word and then a sentence and finally a message or an idea. After doing this for a while, they asked Seth if there wasn't a more efficient way to communicate. He responded that there was, told Jane how she could channel and the rest, as they say, is history.

THE OUIJA BOARD DESCRIBED:

The term Ouija breaks down as Oui, yes in French and ja, yes in German. The ouija board is about eighteen inches by twelve. As you face it, you see an area on the upper left designated as Yes and an area on the upper right designated as No. The alphabet arcs through the centre in two lines, A to M on the first and N to

Z on the second. The numerals 1 through 0 are in a straight line approximately two to three inches from the bottom and the last line, about an inch from the bottom, says Good-bye.

In addition to the board, you need a pointer table. This is a short three-legged, triangular table that measures about an inch in height, about five inches in length and approximately four inches across the base, which is at the opposite end from the point. The table is usually made of wood or plastic and it slides easily on its three legs across the ouija board.

PROCEDURE:

Although it has been known to achieve results with a single operator, the ouija board is usually best operated by two people. To set it up, the two people sit comfortably opposite each other with the board on either a table between them or on the lap of one of them. The pointer table is then placed upon the board and the two operators place their fingers lightly but firmly on the table. This is done without resting their elbows on anything so that the pointer table is able to move around the board freely and easily.

There are a couple of ways to activate the board. One is for the two operators to simply place their fingers on the pointer table and wait. In anywhere from one to five minutes the pointer should begin to move. The other way is to begin by asking questions. Most people regard the Ouija board as a parlour game and tend to ask questions that relate to romance, money and the future. I suggest that you begin with questions that are directed to whatever/whoever is responding, e.g. "Who are you?" Have you ever lived in physical reality or on earth?" "What was your name?" With these kinds of questions, you have more material to evaluate and more information from which you can draw conclusions about the legitimacy of the ouija board.

For best results, it is important that only one person ask the questions and it helps if both individuals concentrate on the content of the questions. Once the ball gets rolling, a question-response rhythm develops and concentration is less necessary.

Sometimes, nothing will happen. This can be for a variety of reasons. Sometimes, one or both of the operators is frighten of the prospect of dealing with a spirit and gets "spooked." Sometimes the attitude of the operators and/or others in the room is frivolous or otherwise not conducive. Possibly, there is no entity immediately available or interested in having such a conversation. I'm sure there are other reasons, so, be prepared for the Ouija not working, but it's probably a better bet to expect that it will work.

As to why this thing works, I really don't know. I have seen it take off and really jump around the board and provide answers that convince me that something outside of my conscious self is operating. Whether it is another entity on its own, another entity operating the two operators' hands or whether it is something within the two operators unconscious that is providing the answers, I really don't know. What I do know is that something beyond the operators' conscious awareness is operating and it can be an interesting source of information.

Regardless of what you believe or irrespective of what is actually directing the pointer, I suggest that you give it a try if you have an interest in pursuing the metaphysical and, who knows, it may lead to someone becoming another Jane Roberts.

4. INTUITION

A TRUE STORY:

I was once in the Municipal Casino in Nice, misspending my youth. I had a few francs, like about ten or twelve. It cost five to get in so I wasn't there to do a lot of gambling, but simply to look around and enjoy the sights and sounds. I knew that the best bets in a place like this were on the European roulette table, where there are three bets where the odds are 19 to 18 in the house's favour. These bets are Red against Black, Odd against Even and one to 18 vs. 19 to 36. On a European roulette table there is only one house number, Zero, as opposed to an American table where the house has Zero and double zero. The extra house number on the American table makes the odds on these three bets rather prohibitive and very much in the house's favour.

Anyway, I decided that I would play these bets as long as my money held out. The minimum bet was two francs and I was just going to hunch my way along, as long as I could. I can't recall the specific bets but my play was based on something like: Red vs. Black, hmm... Black. So, I put my two francs on Black and won.

Now I had four francs and I quickly entertained the second bet. It might have been something like: Even vs. Odd, humm...Odd. The four francs went down on Odd, the wheel spun and I then had eight francs.

This went on for a while. I did not manage my money, as prudent gambling would dictate, I was only interested in seeing how far my luck would run if I just used my gut and hunched my way along. It was doing quite well. I was acquiring a bit of an audience, "Mon Dieu, Monsieur!" and the chips were coming in different colours and shapes.

My undoing came when I started to think. I thought, if I started with two francs, I would stop when I had two hundred dollars — I could have lived off that for a couple of weeks, in the mid 60s, in the south of France. Well, at that time, two hundred dollars was 1024 francs. That meant that my two francs would have to double 9 times. The thinking that undid me was that I had won nine times and, in the excitement of the moment, I miscalculated and thought I had to win one more time. I placed my 1024 francs on the table and ended the night down two francs.

What do you think the odds are of doubling a bet nine times in a row, where the odds are 19 to 18 against you, and winning each time? I forget how to calculate probabilities but the answer is likely astronomical and the chances of repeating such a string of wins is probably impossible in one lifetime. My point in telling you this is that, in that casino, at that time, I used my intuition. I was really in the zone. I was relaxed and floating. For a while, I didn't think, I felt and reacted. It came unravelled when I started to think. Easy money can do that to you.

Suppose you could tap into your intuition anytime you wanted. Well, we can, but most of us have difficulty with this. Usually, our analytical ability or thinking gets in the way and we don't believe our intuition's input. But, if we listen to our intuition and learn to trust it, we are well on our way to developing it. To listen to it, I find it helps to focus on the body. Some think it originates in the heart, some in the gut, and others in the stomach. Thinking comes from the head and, if you focus your attention, you can discern the difference. The little voice from the head is thinking and the little voice from the body is intuition.

INTUITION IN MANAGEMENT:

I recall, years ago, reading an article, in *The Financial Post*, about a scientist, who had worked with NASSA on some telepathy experiments. After NASSA, he developed a model for predicting which presidents of large organizations would be most successful. He had a questionnaire that basically identified those who relied heavily on gut feel or intuition. His hypothesis was that, in those days, and maybe even with microcomputers today, as information travelled upward in a large organization, by the time it reached the top, it was terribly distorted and, when it was used as input for decisions, the CEO was really guessing. His model purported to identify the better guessers and thus the more successful presidents. The better guessers were those who relied more on their hunches and gut feel.

As a handwriting analyst, I have had the opportunity to see the handwriting of many senior managers and top executives. Interestingly, there are frequently strong signs of intuition present along with other traits that you would expect to see in such people, such as good thinking, analytical ability, leadership, etc.

INTUITION IS A SIXTH SENSE THAT CAN BE DEVELOPED.

My point in all of this is that intuition is a sixth sense, we all have it and it can be developed. There are lots of ways to develop one's intuition. One of the best is to buy Laura Day's book, *Practical Intuition*, and go through the exercises that she lays out. This will require time and discipline but it is well worth the effort and takes less time than it does to learn many things that are not nearly as important.

The other way you can develop intuition is to practice using it. Make guesses. When approaching line-ups at a check out area, guess which one will move quickest. When waiting for an elevator, in a row of elevators, guess which one will come first. Go through a shuffled deck of cards and guess which colour will turn up next. Play hunches when it comes to everyday decisions. Do it often and do it quickly. Experiment and play with it and discover what works and what doesn't.

DON'T LET THE MIND GET IN THE WAY.

The key thing is to make your guesses quickly, before thinking can kick in and persuade you that you are wrong. Thinking is the biggest saboteur of intuition. And, of course, in our society, thinking is highly valued whereas intuition is considered to be anti-intellectual or for the more feeble-minded.

Intuition works best when we are relaxed, spontaneous and take note of the information before we think. This doesn't mean that we can't bring thinking to bear later. We were born with both intuition and a mind, and, when making decisions, we should use them both. Certainly, after getting a feeling about something and noting that feeling, it can be quite appropriate to think about it before coming to a conclusion or acting. I think you'll be surprised at how often the original feeling turns out to be valid and useful.

5. PSYCHOMETRY

ANOTHER TRUE STORY:

I once attended a seminar that Anne Morse was putting on at the Learning Annex in Toronto. Anne channels the Transeekers and is a very talented individual. At one point in the evening, Anne asked all of us to place a personal object on a table, and to do it so that the others would not see which objects belonged to which individuals. She then asked us to pick up one object from the table that belonged to someone else and hold it. She asked each of us, in turn, to note any impressions and feelings that we got about the owner of the object and then to describe these aloud for all to hear. If we thought we had some advice for the owner, we were encouraged to include it. After we had all taken our turns at doing this, Anne directed each of us to take a moment and give some feedback to the person who picked up our object and spoke to or about us.

I can't recall what was said about me or very much about what I said. What was memorable was that when the seminar was over, the woman whose ring I had picked up came over and thanked me profusely for what I had said to her. Apparently, she was stuck on some issue and what I told her, she said, was just exactly what she needed to hear.

Well, I was certainly flattered and, momentarily felt very pleased with myself, but I honestly didn't feel that I had done anything very special. The words that I had spoken seemed to me to be a lucky guess. I just spoke about a couple of ideas that came into my mind, and I did it very tentatively, with a great deal of self-consciousness.

ANOTHER ABILITY THAT IMPROVES WITH PRACTICE.

Since then, I have done this, with a few friends, on a number of occasions and have found that some people have a real talent for it. I don't seem as talented as many but, every once in a while, I have a real hit. I suggest you try it. I believe that, with practice, the ability improves and we can glean some interesting information.

DON'T BE TOO QUICK TO DISCARD.

Another point to keep in mind with Psychometry, as well as with other intuition exercises, is that a response or an idea that comes to us, may seem absolutely wrong or inappropriate, or when we say it to someone else, they may express that the reading is wrong or way off base. Interestingly, what at first, may seem off base, often develops real meaning, if given a little time. Or put another way, when we first hear a message from such a reading, we may not be ready or well disposed to hear or understand it but, when some time goes by, we develop a new perspective or disposition and the message suddenly makes perfect sense.

I invite you to try Psychometry. Try it with a few friends and I am sure that you and they will enjoy the experience. As well, you may be pleasantly surprised at what you learn about each other and, of course, it's a fair bet that you will continue the adventure of discovering more about yourself.

6

CONCLUSION & SUMMARY

This book was constructed so that you and I would learn some concepts that would help us to understand how the universe might work and, thus, more about ourselves. Writing it has forced me to wrestle with these concepts, organize them, clarify them and find words to express them so that someone else could make sense of them. Going through that exercise certainly contributed to my understanding and I hope that reading this book has contributed to yours.

The two pages that follow are a summary of the underlying thesis of this book. It is the essence of part one and I hope that it will help us all to recall and reinforce the metaphysical points that I think are the most significant for self-discovery.

SUMMARY:

- God is not a person separate from us but pure consciousness, manifesting as a force that is in everything.
- God has no gender, location, ego, or limits, nor does It need or want the worship of humans.
- God is everywhere, everywhen and everything. It includes all of us as well as all things. There is nothing outside of or separate from God.
- God's purpose is to create and It does so because that is Its nature and because It wishes to experience all that It knows cognitively.
- We are multi-dimensional, holographic aspects/fragments/expressions of All That Is (God).
- We, as a fragment of God, with the full capability of God, are exploring and experiencing different things, in an infinite number of ways, so as to contribute to the overall experiential learning of a higher aspect of ourselves (our oversoul) and ultimately, All That Is/God.
- As we experience and play in this universe of limitation and separation, through many lifetimes, and evolve through the levels of density,
  - We move away from the illusions of limitation and separation.
  - We push back the veil of forgetfulness
  - We expand our awareness
  - We recall more of what we truly are
  - And, thus, we progress back towards the unlimited and unified consciousness or source from which we originated.

- To create this universe, we work with energy and we densify it to varying degrees. The seven major degrees or levels of density are primarily for:
  - Minerals, elements and compounds
  - Most species of plants and animals
  - Humans, primates and cetaceans
  - Humans, peace and Superconsciousness
  - First level of non-physicality
  - The frequency of Christ, Buddah and angels
  - Total oneness and integration
- As we evolve through these levels of density, we are heading home and, because we end up with the understanding that comes from the experiencing of all this, God is richer for the experience.
- As parts of the Infinite Creator, We, have been creating the whole time. This is inherently the nature of God. We have been creating our personalities, our universe, and our whole experience. We are the Creator. Creating is what we do.

And, because creating combined with learning experientially is what we do, then once done, we start off on other adventures, in other universes.

7

BIBLIOGRAPHY

Anka, Darryl, *BASHAR: Blueprint for Change*. SimiValley, California, New Solutions Publishing.1990.

Arka, Srinivas, *Adventures in Self-Discovery*. London, U.K. Minerva Press. 1998.

Benson, Herbert, *The Relaxation Response*. New York, New York. Avon Books. 1975.

Chadwick, Gloria, *Discovering Your Past Lives*. Chicago Illinois. Contemporary Books, Inc. 1988.

Davis, Roy Eugene, *An Easy Guide To Meditation*. Lakemont, Georgia. CSA PRESS, Publishers. 1988.

Day, Laura, *Practical Intuition*. New York, Broadway Books. 1996.

Denning, Melita and Phillips, Osborne, *The Llewellyn Practical Guide to Astral Projection*. St. Paul Minnesota. Llewellyn Publications. 1988.

Denniston, Denise and McWillians, Peter, *The T M Book, How to Enjoy The Rest Of Your Life*. Allen Park, Michigan. Versmonger Press. 1975.

Frissell, Bob, *Nothing in This Book Is True, But It's Exactly How Things Are*. Berkeley, California. Frog Ltd. 1994.

Graves, Tom, *The Elements of Pendulum Dowsing*. Shaftesbury, Dorset, U.K. Element Books Limited. 1989.

Goldsmith, Joel S., *The Art Of Meditation*. New York, N.Y. Harper and Row, Publishers, Inc. 1956.

Hand Clow, Barbara, *The Pleiadian Agenda*. Santa Fe, NM. Bear & Company, Inc. 1995.

Hanson, Peter G, *The Joy of Stress*. Toronto, Canada. Stoddart Publishing Co. Limited. 1986.

Hay, Louise L., *Heal Your Body*. Carson, California, Hay House, Inc. 1988.

Institute For Enlightenment, A Handbook For Humanity. Portland, Oregon. Strawberry Hill Press. 1992.

Kason, Yvonne, *A Farther Shore*. Toronto, Canada. HarperCollins. 1994.

Marciniak, Barbara, Earth, *Bringers of The Dawn*. Santa Fe, NM. Bear & Company, Inc. 1992.

Marciniak, Barbara, Earth, *Pleiadian Keys to the Living Library*. Santa Fe, NM. Bear & Company, Inc. 1995.

McWilliams, Peter, *Life 101*. Los Angeles, California, Prelude Press. 1994.

Moore, Marcia, *Hypersentience*. New York, N.Y., Bantam Books, Inc. 1976.

Paulson, Genevieve Lewis, *Kundalini and the Chakras*. St. Paul, Minnesota. Llewellyn Publications, Inc. 1993.

Pendleton, Don and Linda, *To Dance With Angels*. New York, N.Y. Kensington Publishing Corp. 1990.

Ridall, Kathryn, *Channeling, How to Reach Out to Your Spirit Guides*. New York, New York. Bantam Books. 1988.

Roberts, Jane, *The Coming of Seth*. New York, N.Y. Pocket Books. 1966.

Roberts, Jane, *The Seth Material*. New York, N.Y. Bantam Books. 1972.

Roberts, Jane, *Seth Speaks*. New York, N.Y. Bantam Books. 1974.

Roberts, Jane, *The Nature of Personal Reality*. New York, N.Y. Bantam Books. 1974.

Roberts, Jane, *The Unknown Reality, Volume One*. New York, N.Y. Bantam Books. 1977.

Roberts, Jane, *The Unknown Reality, Volume Two — Part One*. New York, N.Y. Bantam Books. 1977.

Roberts, Jane, *The Unknown Reality, Volume Two — Part Two*. New York, N.Y. Bantam Books. 1977.

Roberts, Jane, *The Nature of The Psyche*. New York, N.Y. Bantam Books. 1979.

Roman, Sanaya and Packer, Duane, *Opening To Channel*. Tiburon, California, H J Kramer Inc. 1987.

Royal, Lyssa & Priest, Keith, *The Prism of Lyra*. Phoenix, Arizona. Royal Priest Research Press. 1992.

Royal, Lyssa & Priest, Keith, *Visitors from Within*. Phoenix, Arizona. Royal Priest Research Press. 1992.

Royal, Lyssa & Priest, Keith, *Preparing for Contact*. Phoenix, Arizona. Royal Priest Research Press. 1993.

Sharamon, Shalila and Baginski, Bodo J., *The Chakra Handbook*. Federal Republic of Germany. Lotus Light Publications. 1991.

Strieber, Whitley, *Communion*. New York, New York. Avon Books. 1987.

Strieber, Whitley, *Transformation*. New York, New York. Avon Books. 1988.

Sutphen, Dick, *Radical Spirituality*. Malibu, CA. Valley of the
Sun Publishing. 1995.

Tyl, Noel, *The Principles and Practice of Astrology, Vols. I to VI*.
Saint Paul, Minnesota. Llewellyn Publications. 1973 to 1974.

Voigt, Anna, *Simple Meditation for everydat relaxation and rejuve-
nation*. Vancouver, B.C. Raincoast Books. 2001.

Walsch, Neale Donald, *Conversations With God, Book 1*. New
York, New York. G.P. Putnam's Sons.1995.

Walsch, Neale Donald, *Conversations With God, Book 2*. New
York, New York. G.P. Putnam's Sons.1997.

Walsch, Neale Donald, *Conversations With God, Book 3*. New
York, New York. G.P. Putnam's Sons.1998.

Webster, Richard, *Spirit Guides & Angel Guardians*. St. Paul,
Minnesota. Llewellyn Publications. 1998.

Zukav, Gary, *The Seat Of The Soul*. New York, New York,
Fireside. 1989.

Also by Peter Dennis

HANDWRITING ANALYSIS
An Adventure in Self-discovery
Third Edition

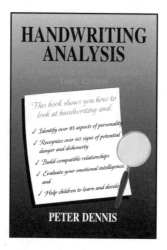

Trade Paperback, 224 pages. ISBN 0-9698926-4-0
Canada $18.95 • U.S.A. $14.95 • U.K. £9.95

**Available online as well as through bookstores
and all major distributors.**

This book will teach you how to look at handwriting and identify over 85 different aspects of human personality. As well, it
will show you how to identify over 60 signs of potential danger
and dishonesty, it will show you how to evaluate your
emotional itelligence, identify who is compatible with whom,
and help parents and teachers contribute more to children's
growth and development. This is a most useful reference for
the fledgling novice and for the experienced analyst.